THE PROLIFERATION SECURITY INITIATIVE:
Making Waves in Asia

Mark J. Valencia

ADELPHI PAPER 376

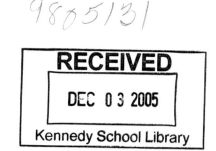
FIRST PUBLISHED OCTOBER 2005
BY **Routledge**
4 PARK SQUARE, MILTON PARK, ABINGDON, OXON, OX14 4RN
FOR **The International Institute for Strategic Studies**
ARUNDEL HOUSE, 13–15 ARUNDEL STREET, TEMPLE PLACE, LONDON, WC2R 3DX
WWW.IISS.ORG

Simultaneously published in the USA and Canada
by **Routledge**
270 MADISON AVE., NEW YORK, NY 10016

Routledge is an imprint of the Taylor & Francis Group

© 2005 THE INTERNATIONAL INSTITUTE FOR STRATEGIC STUDIES

DIRECTOR John Chipman
EDITOR Tim Huxley
MANAGER FOR EDITORIAL SERVICES Ayse Abdullah
COPY EDITOR Jill Dobson
PRODUCTION Jesse Simon
COVER PHOTOGRAPH AFP/Getty

TYPESET BY Techset Composition Ltd, Salisbury, Wiltshire
PRINTED AND BOUND IN GREAT BRITAIN BY Bell & Bain Ltd, Thornliebank, Glasgow

British Library Cataloguing in Publication Data
A catalogue record for this book is available from the British Library

Library of Congress Cataloguing in Publication Data

ISBN 0-415-39512-7
ISSN 0567-932X

CONTENTS

GLOSSARY

ASEAN	Association of South East Asian Nations
BWC	Biological and Toxic Weapons Convention
CARAT	Cooperation Afloat Readiness and Training
CIA	Central Intelligence Agency
CWC	Chemical Weapons Convention
DPRK	Democratic People's Republic of Korea
EEZ	Exclusive Economic Zone
EU	European Union
G-8	Group of Eight Industrialised Nations
IAEA	International Atomic Energy Agency
IISS	International Institute for Strategic Studies
IMO	International Maritime Organisation
JDA	Japan Defense Agency
JMSDF	Japan Maritime Self-Defense Forces
JSDF	Japan Self-Defense Forces
MDA	Maritime Domain Awareness
MOFA	Ministry of Foreign Affairs
NATO	North Atlantic Treaty Organisation
NLL	Northern Limit Line
NORAD	North American Aerospace Defense Command
NPT	Nuclear Non-Proliferation Treaty
PSI	Proliferation Security Initiative
RMSI	Regional Maritime Security Initiative
SEACAT	Southeast Asia Cooperation Against Terrorism
SOLAS	Safety of Life at Sea
SUA	Suppression of Unlawful Acts Against the Safety of Maritime Navigation
UN	United Nations
UNCLOS	United Nations Convention on the Law of the Sea
UNSC	United Nations Security Council
UNSCR	United Nations Security Council Resolution
US	United States
USFJ	US Forces in Japan
WMD	Weapons of Mass Destruction
VBSS	visit, board, search and seizure

Introduction

Experts predict a 70% chance of an attack with nuclear, biological or chemical weapons of mass destruction (WMD) somewhere in the world in the next decade.[1] To keep WMD out of the hands of US-designated 'rogue' states and terrorists, on 31 My 2003, President George W. Bush proposed the Proliferation Security Initiative (PSI) in an address before the Group of Eight (G-8) Summit in Krakow, Poland.[2] In the PSI's own language, this interdiction initiative is an 'activity' designed to prevent the spread of WMD, their delivery systems and related materials from entering or leaving 'states of proliferation concern'. Asia figures prominently in PSI strategy because it contains both suspected suppliers and recipients of WMD-related materials and the main sea and air routes for their transport. Indeed, the first and foremost PSI target is North Korea: the February 2005 US allegation that North Korea supplied Libya with uranium that could be enriched to make nuclear weapons has made the PSI a prominent policy option.[3] In April 2005 the United States indicated that it may step up PSI intercepts of suspect vessels and aircraft bound to and from North Korea as a means of pressuring it to return to the Six-Party Talks involving China, Japan, North Korea, Russia, South Korea and the United States, or if those talks fail.[4]

Some analysts argue that interdiction is critical to preventing the spread of WMD[5] because of the rapid growth in states and groups pursuing WMD programmes, the purported expanding nexus between WMD and terrorism, and the failure of the current non-proliferation architecture.

Interdiction fills the lacunae by ensuring commitments are kept and stops proliferation-related exports by states outside existing non-proliferation regimes. Moreover, it deters suppliers and customers and makes proliferation more costly and difficult.

The Bush administration has high hopes and expectations for the PSI. It made the PSI a key foreign policy and defence goal in 2005, and the US Congress has approved $50 million to help states support the initiative.[6] John Bolton, then US Under-Secretary of State for Arms Control and International Security, and now US Ambassador to the United Nations, proclaimed on 31 May 2004, the first anniversary of the PSI's initiation, that the PSI would evolve to the point where it 'will have shut down the ability of persons, companies or other entities to engage in this deadly trade'.[7] He claimed that the PSI was 'succeeding because it is based on practical actions that make maximum use of each country's strengths to counter proliferation. The partnerships being forged, the contacts being established, the operational readiness being enhanced through PSI are all helping to create a lasting basis for co-operative action against proliferation'.[8] On its second anniversary, in May 2005, US Secretary of State Condoleezza Rice claimed that the United States and its PSI partners had undertaken 11 successful intercepts since its inception, including the prevention of two WMD-related deliveries to North Korea and of ballistic missile-related and nuclear programme-related materials to Iran.[9] These claims of success have been repeated by the new Undersecretary of State for Arms Control and Disarmament, Robert Joseph.[10] However, the details of the intercepts were left vague, partly because some foreign governments were worried about reprisals if they were thought to be cooperating with the United States.[11] Some critics challenged these claims of success, pointing out that there was little public evidence to support the US claim that the PSI was responsible for intercepting the delivery of WMD-related materials to Libya.[12] Indeed some argue that the PSI was not responsible, and that the intercept was part of an unrelated ongoing effort to get Libya to abandon its ambition to possess nuclear weapons.[13]

Although the PSI has indeed made considerable progress,[14] its aggressive promotion and implementation have also created considerable controversy. It has been criticised for lack of transparency, stretching if not violating the principles of international law, weakening the UN system, being ineffective and politically divisive, and diluting other non-proliferation efforts. It has also been cast upon an already stormy maritime security environment.

CHAPTER ONE

The Asian maritime security context

The PSI is being introduced into a politically roiled maritime realm: Asian seas are already fraught with potential flash-points. As coastal states extend their jurisdiction and enforcement seaward, they are increasingly coming face to face with neighbours as well as extra-regional maritime powers that are competing for resources, showing the flag or collecting intelligence. Interpretations of law and conceptions of sovereignty clash, perceptions of threat diverge, and sensitivities are sharpened. The resultant incidents, while seemingly innocuous, often bring to the surface deep-seated fears, unleashing surges of nationalism. Competing claims and related activities in relation to small remote maritime features, like the Northern Territories/ Southern Kuriles, Tok Do/Takeshima, the Senkakus/Diaoyus and the Spratlys, have soured relations between the claimants. The same applies to rival claims to fisheries in the Sea of Japan (East Sea) between Japan and South Korea and to potential oil and gas in the East China Sea between China and Japan. The conflicting claims in the South China Sea have been sources of friction and occasionally international violence for many years, pitting China against ASEAN members and indirectly involving the United States.

Other potential maritime conflict focuses on competition for the control of sea-lanes. These include the Taiwan Strait as an important choke point in its own right regardless of the China–Taiwan imbroglio, and the economically critical Malacca Strait. In the latter case, the interests of China, Japan, India and the United States converge and politically clash – both with each other and with those of the littoral states of Indonesia and Malaysia. The security and control of sealanes through the Indonesian and Philippine archipelagos are also politically contentious.

The rise of maritime security issues in Asia

Maritime issues have risen to the forefront of Asian security concerns since the 1980s.[1] In particular, the 1982 United Nations Convention on the Law of the Sea (UNCLOS) has introduced new uncertainties and conflict points into Asia, particularly with regard to exclusive economic zones (EEZs) and continental shelf claims and boundaries.[2] In Northeast Asia, to avoid confrontation and conflict, unilateral maritime claims have generally not been explicit. But this means that little progress has been made in negotiating bilateral marine boundary agreements. Indeed, only two out of eleven potential boundaries have been defined in the region. In 1974 Japan and South Korea defined their continental shelf boundary for about 260 nautical miles (nm) through the Korea Strait and the western entrance to the Yellow Sea and – more significantly – agreed on the joint development of their overlapping continental shelves in the northern East China Sea. In 1986, North Korea and the USSR (now succeeded by Russia in this context) agreed on their common continental shelf and EEZ boundary.

Potential and actual disputes abound. For example, although North Korea announced in August 1977 an EEZ claim that extends only to the median line, the 1986 agreed boundary between North Korea and Russia apparently extends to the central portion of the Yamato Bank fishing ground and thus would not be acceptable to Japan and South Korea. Three potential boundaries are complicated by serious disputes over ownership of islands: Tok Do/Takeshima between both Koreas and Japan; the Diaoyu/ Senkaku Islands between China and Japan; and the Northern Territories/ Southern Kuriles between Japan and Russia.

Despite the lack of precision in the definition of bilateral marine boundaries, governments have avoided situations with the potential to provoke conflict by controlling the extent of their offshore economic and technological activity. The countries usually use marine areas that clearly belong to them and avoid zones where conflict could arise. These latter areas are thus treated more like political frontiers than political boundaries. For example, China, Japan, Taiwan and South Korea have generally avoided creating tension by limiting prospecting for oil and natural gas to non-disputed sections of the continental margin. The principal exceptions are Chinese and now Japanese exploration in the East China Sea in areas claimed by both.

Military zones have been established by China, North Korea and South Korea, usually when hostilities were occurring or in the face of threats. The Chinese military zone at the head of the Yellow Sea and the North Korean military zones do extend beyond the territorial seas of those countries, assuming those territorial seas are 12nm wide and claimed from reasonable baselines. South Korea has also delineated special maritime zones extending well beyond its territorial waters. However, the concept of security zones extending beyond a state's territorial sea is not sanctioned by the 1982 UNCLOS.

In Southeast Asia, overlaps and disputes are plentiful and many boundaries remain to be resolved. These disputes involve baselines that do not conform to the UNCLOS, claims to EEZs and continental shelves that extend beyond an equidistant line with the opposite or adjacent state, and/or rival claims to islands and the maritime zones they may or may not be able to generate. Disputed areas most likely to cause diplomatic conflict or worse include the eastern Gulf of Thailand (disputed between Vietnam and Cambodia, and Thailand and Cambodia); east Natuna (Malaysia, China and Indonesia); offshore Brunei (Brunei, China, Malaysia and Vietnam); south of the Gulf of Tonkin (China and Vietnam), and the western Sulawesi Sea (Malaysia and Indonesia, Malaysia and the Philippines, and Indonesia and the Philippines). The most complex, difficult and dangerous disputes are those related to overlapping claims by Brunei, China, Malaysia, the Philippines, Taiwan and Vietnam to the Spratly Islands and their attendant maritime space. The disputed area covers most of the central and southern South China Sea. When combined with the other disputes, little of the South China Sea beyond territorial waters is not claimed by more than one country. Nationalism and expectations of oil resources in disputed areas have intensified all these disputes and increased tension in the maritime sphere.

Many emerging security issues in Asia are essentially maritime. Specialists in Asian maritime security list the following maritime problem areas as requiring greater cooperation: piracy, smuggling, illegal immigration, transnational oil spills, incidents at sea, search and rescue, navigational safety, exchange of maritime information, illegal fishing, and management of resources in areas of overlapping claims.[3] While these issues are all maritime safety problems of an essentially civil rather than military nature, addressing environmental and resource protection and illegal activities at sea necessitates that military forces in the region accept broader responsibilities and different priorities, in terms of their operations, training and force structure development.[4] Although many nations in the region are strengthening or initiating coast guards to deal with these issues, navies are likely to take the brunt of these responsibilities for some time to come, either directly or as backup. These concerns, together with perceived requirements for defence self-reliance and force modernisation, are reflected in the significant maritime dimension to current arms acquisition programmes in the region – for example, maritime surveillance and intelligence collection systems, multi-role fighter aircraft with maritime attack capabilities, modern surface ships, submarines, anti-ship missiles, naval electronic warfare systems and mine warfare capabilities. Some of these new capabilities may be perceived as offensive and their deployment in times of tension might run the risk of inadvertently escalating maritime crises.

To this spectrum of maladies has been added the spectre of maritime terrorism and the transport of WMD. New security concerns have stimulated the conflation of civil and military responses, and have increased international uncertainty and tension in the Asian maritime realm.

A clash of sovereignties

A corollary of the growth of post-Second World War nationalism in Asia has been the concern with preserving and even extending the traditional Westphalian notion of sovereignty. This notion of sovereignty considers inviolate the internal affairs of nations. After the 1648 Treaty of Westphalia, the newly created European states enjoyed such sovereignty and profited by the legitimacy and stability it conveyed. Naturally, more recently independent states wish to do the same and thus fiercely guard their Westphalian sovereignty. Indeed, this is the origin of the key Association of South East Asian Nations (ASEAN) principle of non-interference in the internal affairs of fellow member states.

However, the seas have become the latest battlefront in the contest between Westphalian sovereignty and modern reinterpretations of the concept. In the 1970s, when the concept of sovereignty was extended seaward to encompass strategic straits, the maritime powers baulked. Indonesia and Malaysia claimed the Malacca Strait in 1971 as part of their territorial waters (or, more precisely, its archipelagic and territorial waters in Indonesia's case), and thus it fell under their complete sovereignty. In the negotiations leading to the UNCLOS, two competing concepts emerged regarding the navigation regime in straits such as the Strait of Malacca: innocent passage and transit passage. A regime of innocent passage would have allowed Indonesia and Malaysia to retain their sovereignty over the Strait in the sense that any passage prejudicial to their peace, good order and security could be denied.

But for the maritime powers, the Malacca Strait was the shortest and cheapest route between the Indian and Pacific Oceans and they wanted unrestricted passage of their naval and commercial vessels to be absolutely guaranteed. Thus the maritime powers, led by the United States and the then-Soviet Union, pushed through a regime of 'transit passage' in which the passage of vessels and aircraft cannot be impeded or suspended in any circumstances. Singapore – economically and politically dependent on safe, secure and free passage through the Strait – then, as now, sided with the extra-regional maritime powers. Malaysia and Indonesia were left with a sense of unfulfilled sovereignty regarding the Strait.

As a fresh reminder of this 'limited' sovereignty, in the wake of the attacks of 11 September 2001, the US and Indian navies exercised their transit passage rights to escort vessels of 'high value', such as large tankers and warships, through the Strait. The US and Indian patrols in the Strait created suspicion in Southeast Asia regarding their real goals. America's apparent interest in a close military relationship with India suggested that the coordinated Indian and US naval presence in the Strait may not have been intended solely to combat terrorism, but was part of a broader strategy on the part of Washington as well as New Delhi to promote an Indian naval presence in the region with an eye on countering an incipient Chinese naval build-up there. More recently, in 2004, in the face of a resurgence of piracy and frowing concerns about maritime terrorism in the Strait, Japan and the United States offered their assistance to the littoral states. Indeed, it was – incorrectly – reported that the United States was contemplating sending marines to patrol the Strait under a proposed Regional Maritime Security Initiative (RMSI).[5] Malaysia and Indonesia reiterated their sovereignty in the Strait and bluntly refused. Singapore, which was negotiating a framework agreement on security and defence with the United States, strongly supported the proposal.

In a larger context, the United States, Australia and others are increasingly arguing that state sovereignty is not sacrosanct and that external powers have the right to intervene in states that are unable to suppress violent groups, particularly those that pose a danger beyond those nations' borders. Some commentators have called for or claimed that there are criteria for such interventions, such as the state having 'failed' or the purpose being solely 'humanitarian', but none have been agreed between nations or by the United Nations. However, this lack of agreement on criteria for intervention has not prevented the United States, Australia, Israel, Japan and Russia from asserting, and in some cases, acting upon the right to pre-emptive self-defence.

This trend towards pre-emptive self-defence and the clash of sovereignty concepts explains the strong reaction by Indonesia and Malaysia to RMSI. Indonesia and Malaysia also worried that a US military presence in the Straits of Malacca and Singapore could prove counterproductive, bolstering the ideological appeal of extremists and even attracting terrorist attacks. Consequently, Malaysia and Indonesia opposed the proposal as an affront to their sovereignty and competence. Indonesian navy chief Admiral Bernard Kent Sondakh even suggested that the possibilities of terrorism and WMD transit in the Strait were being exaggerated to engender support for an expanded US military presence there.[6] Faced with pressure from extra-regional maritime powers, Malaysia, Indonesia and Singapore moved to head off the perceived possibility of unilateral foreign intervention by agreeing upon trilateral coordinated maritime patrols in the Malacca Strait. However, each state's vessels would patrol its own waters. The first such patrol took place in July 2004.

'Creeping' jurisdiction

Heightened marine awareness and security concerns have also prompted some developing countries to limit the activities of maritime powers in their EEZs. While a foreign vessel has only the right of innocent passage in the territorial sea, which can be suspended for certain infringements of the regime, the maritime powers generally view the 200nm EEZ regime as allowing unrestricted freedom of navigation. However, military activities in coastal states' EEZs were a controversial issue during the negotiations of the text of the UNCLOS and continue to be so in practice. Some coastal states such as Bangladesh, Brazil, Malaysia, India and Pakistan contend that other states cannot carry out military exercises or manoeuvres in or over their EEZs without their consent. On the other hand, the United States and some other maritime powers contend that according to the balance of interests negotiated into the UNCLOS, coastal states cannot unduly restrict or impede the exercise of freedom of navigation and overflight in and over their EEZs, including the conduct of military activities. These different views have already resulted in several incidents in the EEZs of the Asia-Pacific region, such as the US EP-3E incident on 1 April 2001 over China's EEZ and Vietnam's protest against China's live fire exercises in its EEZ.

Misunderstandings regarding foreign military and intelligence gathering activities in EEZs are bound to increase. Maritime powers and regional navies including the United States, China, Japan and India are expanding their activities and their technology is advancing while as coastal states they are placing increasing stress on control of their EEZs. These opposing trends may cause conflict.[7] In particular, intelligence-gathering activities in Asian EEZs are likely to become more controversial and more dangerous. 'This disturbing prospect reflects their militaries' increasing and changing demands for technical intelligence; their robust weapons acquisition programmes, especially increasing electronic warfare capabilities; and the widespread development of information warfare capabilities. Further, the scale and scope of maritime and airborne intelligence collection are likely to expand rapidly over the next decade, involving levels and sorts of activities quite unprecedented in peacetime. They will not only become more intensive, but generally more intrusive, and will generate tensions and more frequent crises' (*ibid.*). If current trends continue, such activities may produce defensive reactions and escalatory dynamics. This is particularly likely in Asia because of its uniquely complicated maritime geography.

Also complicating the potential conflict over the EEZ regime are confusion, stark differences of opinion between maritime and coastal states, and interpretive inconsistencies regarding the details of the regime governing military and intelligence gathering activities in EEZs. Further, new threats like trade in WMD, piracy, and smuggling of drugs and humans encourage states to extend their surveillance and control, even to others' EEZs. Certainly, in the aftermath of 11 September 2001, many nations, the United States and Australia in particular, have increased their scrutiny of both military and commercial aircraft and ships approaching from near and far. Finally, given the myriad boundary disputes and overlapping claims, it is not always clear where one nation's jurisdiction ends and another's begins. These developments imply that certain UNCLOS provisions formulated 25 years ago in a very different political and technological context may be reinterpreted in the light of these new circumstances. Indeed, there is still disagreement regarding interpretations of the relevant UNCLOS provisions, the means of attempting to resolve disagreements, and even whether or not there is a need to resolve such disagreements, which generally relate to the exact presumed meaning of the terms in the Convention as well as the meaning of specific articles. For example, there are differences regarding the meaning of 'freedom' of navigation and overflight in and above the EEZ, that is, whether such freedoms can be limited by certain regulations or whether such freedoms are absolute.

There are differing interpretations regarding the precise meaning of the Convention's phrase allowing 'other internationally lawful uses' of the sea in the EEZ. For example, some argue that it clearly does not include warfare in the EEZ of a non-belligerent, while others would insist that warlike activities are allowed under the right of self-defence. The interpretation of 'other internationally lawful uses' hinges upon interpretations of such terms as 'due regard', 'abuse of rights', 'peaceful use', 'peaceful purpose', and the obligation not to threaten or use force against other countries. In this context, questions arise as to whether some military and intelligence-gathering activities are a lawful exercise of the freedom of navigation and overflight, and whether they are a threat to the peace and security of the coastal countries.

There is also disagreement on how to deal with these uncertainties. Leaving the problem unresolved could be dangerous in the long run. Incidents are multiplying rapidly and even if bilateral arrangements were possible, the rules may differ depending on the countries and circumstances. Despite these disagreements, most analysts agree that international law and state practice are not static. Moreover, they agree that the UNCLOS is unclear regarding the regime governing military and intelligence-gathering activities in the EEZs of other countries. National governments may deal with these matters unilaterally in order to protect their security and other interests. If numerous coastal states were to enact unilateral national legislation prohibiting the exercise of military and intelligence gathering activities in and above their EEZ, then the prohibition against conducting such exercises could become part of customary international law through state practice, despite the opposition of some countries, particularly if those countries are not parties to the UNCLOS.

Failing the unlikely resolution of these issues by the International Court of Justice or the International Tribunal on the Law of the Sea, these disputes must be addressed through a disorderly process whereby countries assert and defend their positions through state practice, followed by protests by disagreeing countries, and eventually by the give and take of diplomatic negotiations. Sooner or later a consensus may emerge, but the process will strain relations and may lead to new restrictions on foreign military and intelligence activities in other states' EEZs – including those related to PSI.

China is a prime example of a state that does not want to allow foreign military activities in its EEZ, presumably including PSI interdictions by foreign navies. On 1 April 2001, the collision between a US navy surveillance EP-3E aircraft and a Chinese fighter raised several questions regarding the legality of military activities in EEZs.[8] The collision took place about 62nm southeast of Hainan in the South China Sea. China said that the US 'spy' aircraft was flying over its EEZ, and that it was endangering its security. Further, China demanded that the United States halt its intelligence-gathering flights off its coast. The United States said that its aircraft was flying over 'international' waters that for navigation purposes are under the regime of 'freedom of the high seas', and was thus enjoying the freedom of overflight. Moreover it maintained that the aircraft was on automatic pilot and that the Chinese fighter caused the collision by swerving into it. And on 7 May 2001, the United States resumed surveillance flights over China's EEZ. Overall, the United States flies more than 400 reconnaissance missions a year close to China.

The UNCLOS does not address this issue directly. One view is that what is not explicitly prohibited by the Convention is permitted. For example, because the Convention expressly prohibits intelligence-gathering activities in territorial seas in Article 19(2) but not in EEZs, such activities are arguably legal. However, it could be also argued that what is not specified is not authorised. Moreover, the United States has not ratified the Convention so it may be argued that it is not entitled to rights defined by the Convention.

It is clear from the UNCLOS and customary international law that US aircraft enjoy the freedom to fly over China's EEZ. But it is not clear that such freedom is absolute. The real question is whether the intelligence-gathering flights are peaceful acts and give due regard to the 'interests' of China in its exercise of freedom of navigation and overflight, and in its management of its EEZ, including surveillance and enforcement of its regulations.

There is also a question regarding the specific activities undertaken by the US EP-3E aircraft involved in the incident. EP-3Es carry advanced signals intelligence equipment to intercept radio and other communications. The aircraft in question may have been searching for signs of Chinese submarine activities by monitoring military communications traffic. This would be a logical part of a larger US effort to monitor Chinese military activity, including advances in submarine warfare, intelligence-gathering and space-launch activities. The aircraft may even have been interfering with and/or altering communications between elements of China's armed forces. If so, this would certainly not be a 'peaceful' use of China's EEZ.

This uncertainty and debate is not confined to China and the United States. Burma, Japan, Thailand, Indonesia, South Korea and Taiwan have extensive air-defence zones. Burma, India and Vietnam have established military warning zones 24nm wide, while Cambodia and Indonesia have declared such zones 12nm wide. Alien warships and military aircraft without permission are prohibited from these waters and airspace, and in the Vietnamese zone other foreign vessels also must secure permission to transit their waters. These 'excessive' claims are constantly being tested by the United States.[9] Indeed on any given day the US navy is exercising its maritime freedoms against an 'excessive' maritime claim somewhere in the world.

While China insists on prior notification for foreign warships to enter its territorial seas, Australia and other maritime nations such as the United States claim the right of innocent passage in foreign territorial seas. In April 2001, three Australian warships en route from South Korea to Hong Kong allegedly wove in and out of China's territorial waters. China, believing that such passage was not 'innocent', demanded that the warships leave China's territorial waters. Analysts speculated that the incident was in part a reaction by China to Australian Prime Minister Howard's support for US President George W. Bush's position on Taiwan. The incident also occurred only a few weeks after the EP-3 incident.

On 24 March 2001, a week before the EP-3E incident, a Chinese frigate closed to within 100m of the *Bowditch*, a US navy survey vessel collecting data in the Yellow Sea, and warned it not to operate in China's EEZ. China believes such activities are a threat to its security and passed legislation in December 2002 that explicitly makes them illegal. A related question is whether any of the activities carried out by such US naval vessels or aircraft can be considered 'scientific research'. If so, according to the UNCLOS, such activities can only be carried out in another country's EEZ for peaceful purposes, and then only with the consent of the coastal state. From these precedents it is clear that any interdiction under the PSI by a foreign military vessel in China's EEZ would draw significant Chinese protests.

Different threat perceptions

It has become apparent that the United States, as the lone superpower, has significantly different threat priorities and perceptions from many other countries, including even its allies and other PSI members. This is particularly so regarding WMD and their proliferation. The main US concerns are that such weapons will enable small, weaker countries to challenge US political hegemony or, worse, enable non-state groups to attack the United States and its overseas installations, such as military bases, and other symbols of its presence. Thus the United States necessarily has a global threat perspective while the perspectives and interests of most other states are more locally focused. For example, South Korea, a US ally but not a participant in PSI, is more concerned with inter-Korean reconciliation than with terrorism and WMD proliferation, despite North Korea's nuclear weapons programme. Indeed, South Korea increasingly sees itself as a regional balancer and stabiliser rather than a frontline player in thwarting terrorism and WMD proliferation.[10]

Perhaps the most vivid manifestation of these different threat perceptions was the response of Indonesia and Malaysia in May 2004 to the US proposal to assist in guarding the security of the Malacca Strait.[11] There are many security concerns in the Strait, including threats to national sovereignty, smuggling (particularly of arms to separatist movements), threats to the environment and fisheries, threats to fishermen by pirates, threats from pirates to foreign and local shipping, and the threat of terrorism against local targets and against foreign commercial and military vessels, as well as the threat posed by trafficking in WMD.

From Malaysia's perspective, threats to its sovereignty are its highest priority,[12] followed by threats posed by illegal immigration, threats to the environment and fisheries by oil spills, and threats to its fishermen (mainly from Indonesian pirates). Piracy against foreign ships, arms smuggling and maritime terrorism are not its highest priorities. Indonesian's perception is somewhat similar in that threats to its sovereignty are paramount, but that is followed by its concern with arms smuggling to Acehnese separatists in north Sumatra.

The maritime powers using the Strait have quite different priorities. Japan is primarily concerned with piracy. And the United States, since 11 September 2001, considers Muslim extremists throughout Southeast Asia as a potential threat to shipping moving through the region. Its worst-case scenario is that a super-tanker will be hijacked or attacked and sunk in the narrowest portion of the Strait, disrupting commercial traffic, including imports of oil to Japan and South Korea, and potentially constraining US naval mobility and flexibility as well. It is also concerned with the potential shipment of WMD through the Strait.[13] Indeed, one of the supposed purposes of the US-proposed RMSI was to put into regional operation the PSI.[14] But WMD are simply not Malaysia's or Indonesia's chief concern, and this contributed to their opposition to the RMSI proposal as initially presented.

Heightened maritime sensitivities

Geopolitical developments and rising nationalism have heightened maritime awareness and sensitivities in Asia. Rising tension between Japan and North Korea, between the two Koreas, and between Japan and China, has spilled into the maritime arena. Indeed several recent maritime incidents in Northeast Asia have drawn policymakers' attention to the maritime sphere and made projected PSI interdictions there ever more sensitive.

The December 2001 Japanese coast guard attack on and the sinking of a North Korean spy vessel in Japan's and China's EEZ with the loss of all hands[15]

This incident indicated how a PSI interdiction of a North Korean ship might play out, as well as some of the consequences. In this incident, North Korea, though denying any link with the ship, called Japan's actions 'piracy' and 'terrorism'. Tokyo said it acted in 'self-defence'. China expressed concern over Japan's use of force. In late 2003, the Japanese government introduced a law into the Diet allowing suspect foreign ships in its EEZ to be arrested, and if they resist, to be fired on with impunity from domestic liability. The UNCLOS, ratified by Japan and China, already allows a nation to board, inspect and arrest a foreign ship in its EEZ to ensure compliance with its laws and regulations. And under the Convention, Japan also has the right of hot pursuit if it suspects a vessel has violated its EEZ laws. But in implementing a new law sanctioning the use of force, Japan may be moving beyond the Convention.

North Korean ships, including intelligence-gathering vessels or those carrying WMD, related materials or their means of delivery, have freedom of navigation in any country's EEZ, including Japan's. Moreover, at the time of its pursuit of the suspected spy ship, the Japanese coast guard vessels thought the boat was a Chinese fishing boat. According to a 1997 decision by the International Tribunal on the Law of the Sea in the case of M/V *Saiga*, in such situations, 'the use of force must be avoided as far as possible, and where force is unavoidable, it must not go beyond what is reasonable and necessary in the circumstances. Considerations of humanity must apply and all efforts must be made to ensure life is not endangered'.[16] It would appear that the force used by Japan, while perhaps not illegal, was not proportionate to the alleged offence. In any case, the liberal use of force could lead to serious incidents between Japan and its maritime neighbours whose vessels frequently fish illegally in its EEZ.

The 29 June 2002 North Korea–South Korea clash in the Yellow Sea[17]

On 29 June 2002, two South Korean navy vessels tried to block two North Korean navy warships and some North Korean fishing boats which had ventured about 2nm south of the disputed Northern Limit Line (NLL). According to South Korea, the North Korean boats fired first. A North Korean navy boat with heavy-calibre weapons sank a South Korean patrol boat, killing five South Korean sailors and wounding 22.[18] A DPRK warship was seen aflame and being towed north across the sea border.

North Korea argued that it had never recognised the NLL, that it had no fishing boats in the area at the time, that it had not fired first, and that the South Korean boats had 'intruded' into its claimed waters.[19] It further maintained that South Korea precipitated the clash by massing warships in the area to mount a 'surprise' attack. North Korea also alleged that the South Korean military did this in order to undermine any chance of reconciliation and then to blame the North for the impasse. The DPRK rejected the US-led UN command's proposal for military talks, stating that it would only hold talks to discuss the maritime border which it declared to lie considerably to the south of the NLL.[20]

South Korea maintained that North Korea had recognised the NLL implicitly by its actions in the area, and when it signed the 1992 Basic Agreement which stipulated that 'areas for non-aggression shall be identical with those over which each side has exercised jurisdiction until the present time'. South Korea insisted that it would maintain and defend the NLL as the de facto maritime border between the two Koreas, with force if necessary.

The incident had political repercussions on the Korean Peninsula and throughout Northeast Asia. On 10 July, the South Korean domestic media charged that the ROK military had covered up a serious incident on 13 June 2002 for fear of the ruling party losing the local elections.[21] On 12 July, it was reported that the South Korean navy effectively admitted that it mishandled the encounter because of 'incorrect field command reports' and fear of North Korea's anti-ship *Styx* missiles, and the defence minister was replaced.[22] However, the 29 June incident caused both South Korea and the United States to back away from contact with Pyongyang.[23]

Chinese intelligence ships in Japanese waters
In May–June 2000, the *Haibing*-723, a Chinese icebreaker and intelligence-gathering ship, circumnavigated Japan on a suspected intelligence-gathering mission.[24] After carrying out a series of intelligence-gathering activities near the Tsushima Strait, the ship sailed north through the Sea of Japan, crossed the Tsugaru Strait three times back and forth, sailed south along Japan's Pacific coast, past the Boso Peninsula, Shikoku and Amami Oshima. The *Dongdiao*-232, a Chinese intelligence ship, had engaged in intelligence-gathering activities in July off Irako-misaki, Aichi Prefecture and south of the Kii Peninsula. For Japan, the 10 November 2004 incursion of a Chinese submarine into Japanese territorial waters was the last straw.[25]

In addition to gathering intelligence by electronic means about the activities of the Japan Self-Defense Forces (JSDF) and the US Forces in Japan (USFJ), China's intelligence-gathering vessels in Japanese waters were also thought to be surveying water temperature, currents and sea-bottom topography for military purposes such as submarine operations. It is also possible that Chinese naval activities in these waters were designed to intimidate the JSDF and test the reaction of the Japanese government, public opinion and the military.

These incursions contributed to a re-think of Japan's perception of China. The Japanese government now considers China a potential threat. It believes China has increased its vigilance against the Japan–US security alliance because of the strengthening of the alliance since 1996, including, in particular, the enactment of the Law Ensuring Peace and Security in Situations in Areas Surrounding Japan.[26] Indeed, Japan considers the deployment of Chinese naval vessels in the East China Sea an indication of Beijing's opposition to the inclusion of Taiwan by Japan and the United States in the scope of 'situations surrounding Japan'. And Chinese analysts point to Japanese Foreign Minister Kono's May 2000 statement that the Senkakus fall within the security treaty's application.[27] Moreover, Japan thinks the deployment of China's naval vessels may be designed to show China's displeasure and thus discourage Japan and Taiwan from introducing a Theater Missile Defense system, or Taiwan from moving towards independence.

Chinese research vessels in Japan's claimed EEZ (pre-PSI)
Scientific research in another country's EEZ is not usually considered a security issue. But when the countries in question are rivals for power and leadership, as in Northeast Asia, such activities may become infused with nationalism and accentuate the potential for conflict. Since 1998, Chinese marine research as well as navy ships have been frequenting parts of the East China Sea claimed by Japan, causing great concern and consternation in Tokyo. Indeed, Japan claims that these activities include collection of data for military purposes as well as exploration for natural resources – both in violation of the UNCLOS.[28] China argued that it was conducting research in its claimed EEZ and on its claimed continental shelf, which is allowed by the Convention.

Chinese research vessels were sighted on 16 occasions in 1998, 30 times in 1999 and 24 times in 2000 operating within Japan's claimed EEZ in the East China Sea.[29] In 1999, four sightings occurred within the 12nm territorial waters of the disputed Diaoyu/Senkaku islands. Although Japan's Maritime Safety Agency asked the vessels to cease their research and leave the area, they refused. The Chinese activities were concentrated near the Amami islands and some involved magnetic and seismic exploration for hydrocarbons, while others may have been focused on collecting oceanographic data important for submarine operations. No Chinese navy vessels were observed in Japan's EEZ after July 2000. However, one intelligence ship entered Japan's EEZ near Minamidaitou island.[30]

Japan suspects that the increasing activities of Chinese marine research vessels on the Japanese side of the Japan–China equidistant line are designed to make such activities a fait accompli that China can use to its advantage in negotiating the boundary of its EEZ and its continental shelf.[31] Japan is concerned because the major sea lane for tankers importing its vital oil runs through the East China Sea. In mid-2000 these intrusions raised hackles in Japan's ruling Liberal Democratic Party and forced Japanese Foreign Minister Yohei Kono to urge China to curb its operations in Japan's claimed EEZ.[32] Moreover, Japanese lawmakers threatened to postpone a $161m loan to China because of concern among ruling party lawmakers with Chinese 'spy' ships.

On 13 February 2001, Japan and China agreed on a mutual prior notification system.[33] The agreement cleverly avoids specifying any line beyond which advance notification is required. It simply says that China is to give Japan at least two months notice when its research ships plan to enter waters 'near Japan and in which Japan takes interest' and that similarly, Japan is to inform China before its vessels enter waters 'near' China. The notification must include the name of the organisation conducting the research, the name and type of vessels involved, the responsible individual, the details of the research, such as its purpose and equipment to be used, the planned length of the survey, and the areas to be surveyed. Despite this agreement, in 2001 there were at least five 'violations' by China in the East China Sea. This agreement and the sensitivities surrounding it would make a Japanese PSI interdiction of a non-Japanese flagged vessel by the Japan Maritime Self Defense Forces (JMSDF) in this area very dangerous.

In Asia, the PSI is being introduced into an increasingly contested maritime security environment. Readjustments to the new post Cold War reality, China's rise, and Japan's re-emergence as a 'normal' power provide the political backdrop to maritime security concerns. National marine awareness is increasing and jurisdiction and its enforcement are being extended and enhanced. Sovereignty, security concerns and threat perceptions are becoming intertwined, raising sensitivities. PSI interdictions may exacerbate these political differences and sensitivities.

CHAPTER TWO

The Proliferation Security Initiative

Origin and intent of the PSI

The PSI grew out of the US government's implementation of its National Strategy to Combat Weapons of Mass Destruction.[1] That strategy calls for a comprehensive approach to prevent hostile states and terrorists from obtaining WMD and specifically identifies interdiction as the key focus. Interdiction was considered a key tool because proliferators circumvent export controls, sometimes by trading with each other, and establish front companies to 'deceive legitimate firms into selling them WMD-related materials and ship WMD-related materials under false or incomplete manifests'.[2] The PSI is also a 'gap-filler' in the Missile Technology Control Regime (MTCR).[3] This regime of 35 countries attempts to control the spread of technology needed to build missiles that could carry WMD; however, the technology already has spread well beyond its members. Thus, the only real means of control left is interdiction, which is incorporated in the PSI. The PSI is also consistent with international declarations, such as the United Nations Security Council (UNSC) Presidential Statement of 1992, the June 2003 Group of 8 Industrialised Countries' Declaration on the Nonproliferation of Weapons of Mass Destruction, and the European Union–US Joint Statement on the Proliferation of Weapons of Mass Destruction of 25 June 2003.[4]

The original PSI proposal of May 2003 involved assembling a maritime coalition of states willing to agree to selective interdiction of ships bound to or from 'rogue' states – including, in addition to North Korea,

Iran, Sudan, Syria and Cuba.[5] Libya was on the original list, but because it renounced WMD in December 2003, it may no longer be considered a 'rogue' nation.[6] However, some analysts claim credibly that the PSI was and is aimed primarily at North Korea, at least while Pyongyang remains a 'threat'.[7] To counter this perception and thus avoid immediately alienating Russia and China, which are the DPRK's supporters, John Bolton, who was the Bush administration's point-man for PSI, emphasised that the PSI is a global initiative designed to deal with a global problem.[8]

As a follow-up to the Bush proposal, mid- to senior-level officials from Australia, France, Germany, Italy, Japan, the Netherlands, Poland, Portugal, Spain, the United Kingdom and the United States met in Madrid in mid-June 2003 to discuss it. At that time, the United States elaborated the proposal to include interdicting suspect vessels and aircraft on and over the high seas and within or above cooperating states' territorial and archipelagic waters. The United States said it wanted PSI countries to search planes and ships carrying suspect cargo and to seize illegal weapons or missile technologies.

The 11-member group met again in Brisbane on 9–10 July 2003. The Brisbane Conference focused on defining actions necessary collectively or individually to interdict movement of WMD, missiles, or related materials and equipment by sea, in the air or on land. The PSI was reportedly welcomed by participant states as a necessary and innovative approach to the problem of countries that cheat on their international obligations, refuse to join existing regimes and do not follow international norms, and of non-state actors seeking to acquire WMD.[9]

It was – and remains – unclear whether the initiative would use existing international law, or whether there would be attempts to change international law to accommodate it. At present, PSI actions are supposed to be undertaken 'consistent with existing international law and frameworks'.[10] However, at the Brisbane Conference, a divergence of views on this matter appeared within the group, with one faction led by the United States and Australia pushing to set up 'some other structure outside the formal system'.[11] Indeed, Bolton, the leader of the US delegation, said that 'where there are gaps or ambiguities in our authorities, we may consider seeking additional sources for such authority, as circumstances dictate. What we do not believe, however, is that only the Security Council can grant the authority we need'.[12] Paul O'Sullivan, a deputy secretary in the Australian Department of Foreign Affairs and Trade, and Chairman of the Brisbane Conference, said that 'there is a need for some other structure outside the formal system … they are still in the early stages of developing the idea, and some legislation could be adjusted'.[13] Australian Foreign Minister Alexander Downer recognised that there is a 'very real difficulty in terms of vessels that might be going through the high seas because international law requires that those ships should not be intercepted', and that there might be a need for 'some change to international law to facilitate these types of interdictions'.[14] Earlier, on 13 August 2003, US Deputy Secretary of State Richard Armitage said 'we ourselves haven't hit on the total complete answer to our questions about liability and about international legal issues'. [15]

Regarding the legal authority for the PSI, then US National Security Advisor Condoleezza Rice said on 2 November 2003 that 'we are also seeking ways to expand those authorities'.[16] In her new capacity as Secretary of State she stated in June 2005 that 'participants are also considering how these existing [national and international laws] might be strengthened.[17] However, Bolton had already stated that 'we are prepared to undertake interdictions right now, and, if that opportunity arises, if we had actionable intelligence and it was appropriate, we could do it now'.[18] He had further asserted that the countries concerned had reached an agreement authorising the United States to take action on the high seas and in international air space. Indeed, the United States insists that the boarding of ships is permitted if there is 'reasonable cause'.[19] On 2 December 2003, Bolton again asserted that the United States and its allies are willing to use 'robust techniques' to stop rogue nations from getting the materials they need to make WMD – including interdicting and seizing such 'illicit goods' on the high seas or in the air. These remarks were reportedly cleared by US Secretary of State Colin Powell and senior White House officials.[20] And in October 2005, at a meeting in London of PSI core participants, it was agreed that the PSI is aimed at preventing transfers of WMD and related material 'at any time and in any place'.[21] Indeed, Bolton views the PSI as going beyond national criminal provisions and ineffective international export regimes and engaging in actual interdictions.[22]

In November 2004 Paul McHale, US Assistant Secretary of Defense for Homeland Defense, said that maritime defence would focus on being able to 'identify, intercept and defeat weapons of mass destruction' on the high seas: 'We have to forward deploy our maritime defenses, our surveillance capabilities, our surface combatants with the right kinds of operational capabilities to detect and defeat [the enemy] on the seas, ideally hundreds of nautical miles from our coasts'.[23] He added that the PSI gives US Northern Command officials an important interdiction requirement that will extend out to 500nm in the Pacific and 1700nm in the Atlantic. Australia seemed to follow suit, announcing in December 2004 a 1,000nm 'Maritime Identification Zone'. In this zone, Australia asserted the right to require ships bound for its ports to identify themselves, their route, crew and cargo,[24] and to request the same information from vessels transiting its EEZ. Although an Australian official denied that non-compliant vessels would be interdicted, it was not clear what action Australia would take if a suspect vessel continued its course towards the Australian coast or through its EEZ.[25] Australia subsequently abandoned its plan to establish the zone because it belatedly and reluctantly realised that it had no legal authority to enforce it.[26]

The United Kingdom was initially surprised by the US interpretation and intentions: its representative at the July 2003 Brisbane Conference said that all eleven participants agreed that any action taken under the PSI would need to be consistent with international law. Others in the PSI coalition felt that the United States was moving too quickly and too aggressively for them.[27] Indeed, at the extreme there were concerns that the proposal could evolve into a multinational force roaming the seas and skies in search of transporters of illegal or undesirable weapons. To underscore this concern, Javier Solana, the European Union's 'foreign minister', said 'The fight against terrorism, in which the EU is fully engaged, has to take place within the rules of international law'.[28] After the Brisbane meeting, a team from the eleven PSI nations was assigned to work on reaching a consensus regarding the relevant principles of international law.

In early September 2003, the eleven PSI core participants met in Paris and agreed to abide by a set of Interdiction Principles for the Proliferation Security Initiative.[29] These Principles purport to be a step in the implementation of the UN Security Council Presidential Statement of January 1992, which states that the proliferation of all WMD constitutes a threat to international peace and security and underscores the need for member states to prevent proliferation.[30] However, the Principles are not legally binding.

The PSI seeks cooperation from any state whose vessels, flags, ports, territorial waters, airspace or land might be used for proliferation purposes by states and non-state actors of proliferation concern. The PSI participants are committed to the following Principles in order to impede and stop shipments of WMD, their delivery systems and related materials flowing to and from states and non-state actors of proliferation concern, consistent with national legal authorities and relevant international law and frameworks, including the UN Security Council:

- undertake effective measures to interdict the suspected transfer or transport of WMD from 'states or non-state actors of proliferation concern';

- streamline procedures for rapid exchange of relevant information and maximise coordination for interdiction efforts;
- review and strengthen national legal authorities and work to strengthen international law to support interdiction efforts; and
- take specific actions to prevent WMD proliferation by intercepting suspected cargoes at transit points within, or without, national jurisdiction.[31]

There are or were three types of PSI participants: the core group of eleven which founded the arrangement and formulated the Principles; those who subsequently publicly acceded to the Principles; and a group of 'supporters' whose identity and degree of participation are unknown. In August 2005, the Bush administration dismantled the core group because, according to new Under-Secretary for State for Non-Proliferation and International Security, Robert Joseph, it 'has done its job and we have now moved away from it'. [32] He explained that, having defined the basic principles of interdiction, the maintenance of the core group was no longer necessary.

The United States wants all nations to endorse these Principles publicly through a diplomatic note accompanied by a public statement of support.[33] Although it claims that some 60 countries support the PSI, only about 20 have publicly declared such support. Some, perhaps many, of the 40 'behind-the-scenes' supporting countries are tacitly saying that their national interests are at variance with the PSI, while others may be making a gesture of political support without becoming actively or formally involved.[34] For both domestic and international political reasons, or out of fear of becoming a terrorist target, some do not want to be seen to be 'caving in' to the United States. And even of the 20 nations that publicly support PSI, the United States acknowledges that their involvement in actual interdictions will differ according to national capacity and political decisions, as well as their perception of whether or not participation in an interdiction is consistent with their interests, domestic law and international law.[35]

There are at least three levels of substantive activities important to PSI:

- Meetings to engage, discuss and agree to goals, methods, technologies and practices to stop the flow of WMD, related materials and their delivery vehicles.
- Training exercises to broaden international cooperation and skills in detecting shipments and conducting operations to seize WMD and their delivery vehicles during shipment. These exercises may be 'table top' or Command Post Exercises to hone skills in command

and control, intelligence-sharing and evaluation. These exercises may also be international cooperative demonstrations to train deployed forces and enhance interoperability.

- Actual seizure operations.[36]

PSI participants (as opposed to supporters) also agree to: identify national points of contact and internal processes developed for this expanded goal; develop and share national analyses of key proliferation actors and networks, their financing sources and other support structures; and undertake national action to identify law enforcement authorities and other tools or assets that could be brought to bear against efforts to stop a proliferation facilitator.[37]

PSI interdictions and seizures have been ongoing since the initative's inception. Indeed, shipping industry analysts say the United States is stopping and searching vessels at will.[38] Bolton and other Bush administration officials have acknowledged that several seizures have been made under the PSI, but maintain that the details must be kept secret.[39] In March 2004, it was revealed that US Secretary of Defense Donald Rumsfeld had issued a classified order to the US Navy to incorporate terrorism and WMD scenarios into their maritime interception training.[40] The purpose is to prepare all US navy assets to interdict, search, and if necessary, defeat WMD threats. The purported authority for such action is the right of self-defence under Article 51 of the UN Charter.

PSI training activities focus mainly on exercises and simulations developed by an operational group of experts (OEG), which has been meeting quarterly since July 2003, when PSI participants agreed on an initial series of ten sea, air and ground interdiction training exercises.[41] The first official multilateral PSI exercise was *Exercise Pacific Protector*, held 13–14 September 2003 in the Coral Sea, including ships from Australia (destroyers and a customs vessel), Japan (a coastguard patrol vessel) and the United States (the destroyer USS *Curtis Wilbur* and a coast guard Law Enforcement Detachment boarding team) and a maritime patrol aircraft from France. Observers from the other PSI members were supposed to be present. The exercise was aimed at sending a 'sharp signal to North Korea'.[42] Specifically, it was designed to test the mechanics of multinational interdiction on the high seas – the ability of ships and aircraft from different countries to work together to intercept and search a vessel at sea. In October 2003, Spain led a three-day PSI exercise in the Mediterranean, also involving ships and aircraft from France, Germany, Italy, Portugal, the United Kingdom and the United States. The exercise, SANSO-03, was designed to improve joint capabilities for searching merchant ships for WMD.[43] In November 2003, France led a maritime training exercise, BASILIC 03, also in the Mediterranean, which involved seven coalition members as participants or observers.[44]

Six more exercises were carried out in the Middle East and Europe, including both military and law enforcement assets: an Italian-led air interdiction training exercise in the Mediterranean Sea in December 2003; a US-led maritime interdiction exercise in the Arabian Sea in January 2004; a Polish-led ground interdiction exercise in April 2004; an Italian-led aviation interdiction exercise in the Mediterranean Sea in February 2004; a French-led simulated air interdiction exercises in March 2004; and a German-led exercise in March 2004.[45]

A plenary[46] of PSI core participants was convened in London on 9 October 2003 to discuss ways of strengthening the PSI and broadening support for it.[47] In particular, they simulated the interception of a flight suspected of carrying WMD, and exchanged views on a possible boarding agreement presented by the United States. Following this plenary, the eleven original nations plus five new PSI members – Canada, Denmark, Norway, Singapore and Turkey – held an OEG meeting in December 2003 in the United States.[48] The participants analysed the legal authority for interdictions and defined gaps that may be filled through national legislation or international action.[49] They also planned future exercises including *Sea Saber*, conducted in January 2004 in the Arabian Sea. This US-led exercise involved seven active participants, including for the first time a Singaporean naval vessel,[50] and five observer nations out of the then 16 PSI members. In some ways, the exercise mimicked a December 2002 seizure of a shipment of North Korean *Scud* missiles bound for Yemen.[51] The next exercise was hosted by Italy and focused on air interdictions.[52] The coalition convened again in Portugal in early 2004.[53] In October 2004, Japan hosted an exercise codenamed *Samurai 04*. In November 2004, the United States hosted the largest-yet PSI exercise called *Checkpoint 2004*,[54] in the Caribbean; this added the interception of drug smuggling, thought by the United States to be a major source of North Korea's foreign exchange. In March 2005, an OEG group including representatives of 20 nations met at Offutt Air Force Base in Nebraska to discuss ways and means of stopping the movement of WMD. The OEG is considering how to involve new participants, make scenarios more realistic, and enhance expertise and interoperability.[55] In June 2005, it was announced that Iraq, Georgia and Argentina had declared their commitment to the PSI Principles,[56] and thus have become PSI core participants.

In July 2005, Denmark hosted a OEG meeting in Copenhagen focusing on air interdictions.[57]

In April 2005, Portugal hosted a maritime/ground exercise and Spain hosted another exercise in June 2005. Also in early June 2005, an exercise called *Bohemian Guard 2005* was conducted by Bulgaria, Croatia, the Czech Republic, Hungary, Latvia, Poland, Romania, Slovakia, Ukraine and the United States.[58] It focused on intercepting a simulated rail shipment of chemical weapons-related materials as it transited from Poland through the Czech Republic. Singapore hosted a PSI drill in the South China Sea in August 2005 involving 13 countries.[59] There have been about 17 multinational exercises so far. More than 40 countries have participated in one or more of the PSI exercises or simulations. Some 15 sea, air and land exercises have been planned for 2005–06[60] including one to be hosted by Turkey.

A multilateral exercise that involved PSI-like activities but which had no publicly acknowledged link to PSI was held under the auspices of the 3rd Western Pacific Naval Symposium in Singapore in May 2005. The exercise included the sharing of a 'sea situation' system among 19 navies. The system, known as ACESS, can be used to detect, identify and trace ships of interest.[61] The exercise was one of the most complex to date, and focused on a Middle East-bound Libyan-flagged tanker, the *M/V Avatar*, which intelligence indicated was carrying WMD-related materials. After searching 600 square nautical miles, the tanker was located about 185km northeast of Singapore in the South China Sea. The vessel was asked to stop and allow boarding. The master refused and Singaporean commandos rappelled onto the ship and secured the vessel. The vessel was searched and a suspicious container was located. The vessel was escorted to the Pasir Panjang Port where the container was unloaded and found to contain eight metal drums of unknown material. The material was sampled and tested.[62]

Also possibly related to PSI is the annual Southeast Asia Co-operation Against Terrorism (SEACAT) exercises organised by the US Navy in the Philippine and South China Seas.[63] During the 2005 exercise the Indonesian, Philippine, Singaporean and Thai navies conducted visit, board, search and seizure (VBSS) exercises on 'rogue ships'. Meanwhile, the US and Singaporean navies launched the first phase of the annual Co-operation Afloat Readiness and Training (CARAT), conducted from June through August 2005 with six Asian nations including, for the first time since 2002, Indonesia.[64] For the first time, search and seizure were introduced into the CARAT exercise.

Since the original US proposal in May 2003, formal participation in PSI has grown from a core of eleven mostly Western nations to more than 20 states, but these include only four Asian nations. Although the United States claims that there are at least 40 other PSI supporters, it refuses to identify them, leaving some doubt as to the depth and breadth of their commitment and participation. The participants have formulated a set of principles regarding interdictions, and exercises and experience continue to expand in number, nature and participation.

The PSI has developed rapidly, but it is not clear how many more adherents it will attract, and how effective it has been, or will be. The types of materials interdicted are unknown and could be simple supporting technologies like computers or dual-use substances or equipment. Moreover, one analyst argues that compared to the average of 64.5 incidents a year of detected illicit nuclear trafficking between 1991 and 2001 reported by the Stanford Database on Nuclear Smuggling, Theft and Orphan Radiation Sources, eleven interdictions in nine months is a very poor result.[65] This comparison implies that the interdictions are capturing only a small fraction of WMD, delivery mechanisms and related materials actually being moved internationally.

Relevant specific incidents

The following incidents were either carried out under the auspices of the PSI or are relevant to it because of the lessons learned.

The Ku Wol San

One of the incidents most relevant to the PSI occurred on 30 June 1999 in the port of Kandla in northwest India. According to the *Washington Post*, 'after a melee, Indian customs agents managed to board the *Ku Wol San*, a North Korean freighter. Hidden inside wooden crates marked "water refinement equipment" was an alleged assembly line for ballistic missiles: tips of nose cones, sheet metal for rocket frames, machine tools, guidance systems and, in smaller crates, reams of engineers' drawings labelled "Scud" and "Scud C". Documents from the investigation contained a partial list: components for missile sub-assembly; machine tools for setting up a fabrication facility; instrumentation for evaluating the performance of a full missile system; and equipment for calibrating missile components. In other boxes, inspectors found personal items apparently intended for North Korean workers, including cookbooks in Korean, Korean spices, pickles and acupuncture sets. A separate cargo bay contained rocket nose cones, stacks of metal pipe and heavy-duty presses used for milling high-grade steel. Inspectors found a plate-bending machine capable of rolling thick metal sheets; toroidal air bottles used to guide warheads after separation from a missile; and theodolites, devices that measure missile trajectories. It was an intriguing mix, far different from other previously seized shipments because it contained more than just missile engines and spare parts. A technical committee of Indian missile experts concluded that the equipment was "unimpeachable and irrefutable evidence" of a plan to transfer not just missiles, but missile-making capability. The cargo "points to one and only one end-use, namely the assembling of missiles and manufacture of the parts and subassemblies of surface to surface missiles", the technical panel wrote in its report. Although Indian officials insisted that the cargo was intended for Pakistan, US and South Korean officials think it was bound for Libya.'[66]

Previous US-led or inspired interdictions

Several US-led maritime monitoring and interdiction initiatives have been in operation since the beginning of the wars in Iraq (1991) and Afghanistan (2001). These include the *Maritime Interdiction Operation* in the Arabian Sea and NATO's *Operation Active Endeavor* and the *Leadership Interdiction Operation*, both begun in 2001, in the eastern Mediterranean. The *Maritime Interdiction Operation* is based on UN resolutions against Iraq, while the *Leadership Interdiction Operation* and *Operation Active Endeavor* target al-Qaeda and Taliban-linked operatives.[67] Since *Operation Active Endeavor's* inception, more than 61,000 merchant vessels have been queried and 85 have been boarded.[68] In December 2001, not long after the events of 11 September, the Royal Navy detained a London-bound vessel, the M/V *Nisha*, in international waters on suspicion of carrying a 'terrorist cargo'.[69] None was found.

On 21 March 2003, as the war on Iraq began, the US Navy's Liaison Office issued a notice to all shipping in the eastern Mediterranean, Red Sea, Arabian Sea, Gulf of Oman, and Arabian Gulf that warned 'all maritime vessels or activities that are determined to be threats to coalition naval forces will be subject to defensive measures, including boarding, seizure, disabling or destruction, without regard to registry or location'.[70] Indian–US joint naval exercises beginning in October 2003 have also included visit, board, search and seizure (VBSS) operations.[71] As part of *Operation Active Endeavor*, in May 2003, NATO naval forces in the eastern Mediterranean boarded four vessels they believed to have links to terrorists or illegal activities.[72] The ships flew Syrian, Georgian and Comoros flags. No evidence of illegal activity was found. Canadian naval vessels participating in *Operation Apollo* with the US-led coalition fleet in the Arabian Gulf hailed nearly 1,900 ships between September 2001 and September 2004, of which 136 were boarded for closer inspection.[73] The United States and its allies continue to conduct maritime interception operations on the high seas in these areas.[74]

Since September 2001, Western intelligence experts have compiled a list of 20 high-priority ships which are suspect because of their trading patterns or frequent changes in flags or owners.[75] And NATO has decided to allow boarding of suspect ships, provided the ship's master agrees. If the master does not agree, NATO warships will ensure the vessel is inspected as soon as it calls at a 'friendly' port.

The So San

Given the frustration and controversy within the US government and the timing of the initiation of the PSI, this incident was probably the immediate progenitor of the PSI. On 9 December 2002, the US navy observed a vessel in the Western Indian Ocean with a painted-out North Korean flag on the ship's funnel. The Korean characters for 'So San' were freshly painted on the hull, and the vessel was flying no flag. The US government, which had tracked the *So San* from a North Korean port, asked the Spanish navy, which was participating in *Operation Enduring Freedom* at that time, to check on the vessel. When queried by the Spanish naval vessel, the *So San's* master replied that the vessel was registered in Cambodia, and carrying a cargo of cement for Socotra Island, Yemen. However, no ship by the name 'So San' was recorded in the international register of ships. The Cambodian government was requested to confirm the master's claim of nationality, and if nationality was confirmed, to authorise a boarding of the ship to examine the ship's papers, question the persons on board and search the vessel. The Cambodian government confirmed that a ship meeting the description of the vessel was registered in Cambodia under the name 'Pan Hope'. Based on this conflicting information, the Spanish navy suspected that the vessel was 'stateless' (that is, operating without any country's authority) and decided to board; however, the *So San* manoeuvred evasively. The Spanish warship *Navarra* then fired warning shots and rapellers boarded the ship from helicopters.

Once on board, the boarding party inspected the ship's papers, which indicated the vessel was indeed registered in Cambodia. The ship's manifest indicated that the cargo was 40,000 bags of cement. About two dozen 4.5m × 13m sealed containers were observed that were not listed on the cargo manifest. The boarding party opened the containers and found 15 *Scud* missiles.[76] Elsewhere in the hold they found 24 tanks containing a rocket-fuel additive and 100 barrels of unidentified chemicals.

The US navy took control of the vessel from the Spanish. Yemen protested that it had legitimately purchased the missiles from North Korea for its own defence. Washington reluctantly released the vessel and its cargo for transfer to Yemen. When queried about this case, Ari Fleisher, the then White House Spokesman, stated that the ship was boarded because it 'was an unflagged vessel' but permitted to proceed to Yemen because 'there is no provision under international law prohibiting Yemen from accepting delivery of missiles from North Korea'. Fleisher stated further that 'while there is authority to stop and search, in this instance there is no clear authority to seize the shipment of Scud missiles from North Korea to Yemen and therefore the merchant vessel is being released'.[77]

Boarding a ship to verify its nationality is allowed under the internationally recognised right of visit,[78] and there was sufficient doubt in the case of the *So San* (e.g., the painted-out ship's name, the lack of a flag). However, doubts as to a ship's nationality do not provide a legal basis to search it for WMD, nor is there any law prohibiting the transport of conventional arms. Because the boarding was conducted in accordance with international law, the North Korean claim that it was an act of piracy is groundless. In any case, as North Korea denied it was the flag state, it had no standing to raise this complaint. However, any claims that the ship was a 'piratical ship' simply because it was not showing a flag and was carrying a false or incomplete cargo manifest are also inaccurate. Indeed, if the flag state was known and refused permission for boarding, doing so could have been considered an 'act of war'. Moreover, the United States is not at war with the flag state so any claim that the vessel and cargo were subject to capture as contraband or a prize is unconvincing. Most importantly, any claim that the ship could have been seized as an act of self-defence is unsupported because there was no evidence that the missiles were to be used in an imminent attack on the United States.

The Ville de Virgo

In April 2003, the *Ville de Virgo*, a French-owned ship carrying 214 aluminium tubes that could serve as gas-centrifuge components for enriching uranium for nuclear bombs, was intercepted based on tips from French and German intelligence agencies as it was entering the northern end of the Suez Canal.[79] The shipment, procured in Germany and unloaded in the Egyptian port of Alexandria, was destined for North Korea. German police arrested the owner of a small export company and said they had uncovered a scheme to acquire up to 2,000 such pipes. Investigators said they had concluded that that amount of aluminium could have yielded about 3,500 gas centrifuges for enriching uranium. A Western diplomat said the intentions 'were clearly nuclear'. The result could have been several bombs' worth of weapons-grade uranium in a year.

Singapore incident

In May 2003, a ship, loaded with 33 tons of sodium cyanide, a chemical that can be used in the manufacture of the deadly nerve agent tabun (purchased in Germany, one of the world's leading producers and exporters of toxic gas) was arrested and inspected in Singapore before reaching Pyongyang. Although there are few details about this incident, it does indicate that PSI interdictions include dual-use materials.

The Baltic Sky

On 24 June 2003, Greece sent commandos to seize the cargo ship *Baltic Sky* in Greek territorial waters. The vessel was carrying 750 tons – a huge amount – of industrial-grade explosives and detonators from Tunisia to Sudan. The ship had wandered around the eastern Mediterranean for six weeks after picking up its cargo in Tunis. NATO alleged that the ship, initially thought to be Comoros-flagged but later determined to have been removed from the Comoros registry, was operating in an abnormal and suspicious manner. However, authorities in Tunis and the cargo buyer in Khartoum claimed that the purchase and transport of the explosives were legitimate. The Greek authorities may have considered that allowing the *Baltic Sky* to transport such a dangerous cargo through its territorial waters violated the UNCLOS provision for innocent passage because it was prejudicial to Greece's security and 'good order'. The captain and six crew members were detained and charged with illegal possession and transportation of explosives.[80] Police said they were looking into the possibility that the vessel was being used in a sting operation to entrap terrorists who might try to buy its cargo.[81]

The Daewoo incident

On 1 July 2003, Spanish forces seized a ship carrying Daewoo-manufactured rifles and 100mm guns from Busan in South Korea to Senegal. The South Korean Defence Ministry protested that the shipment of 280 K1 machine guns and 100 K2 rifles was legal. However, it added that other weapons in the cargo, such as Kalashnikov assault rifles, may have been smuggled onto the freighter to be exported to a third country, most likely, the Ivory Coast.[82] This incident demonstrates how widely the interdiction net has been cast.

The Be Gaehung

In August 2003, hazardous chemicals were seized from a 6,500-ton North Korean freighter, the *Be Gaehung*, in Kaohsiung port, Taiwan.[83] In this case,

Taiwanese law enforcement authorities were alerted by US intelligence. Despite strong protests from the ship's crew, local authorities boarded the ship and seized 158 barrels of phosphorous pentasulfide, which is an additive in motor oil and an ingredient of insecticide, but which also can be used to make nerve gas.

The BBC China incident

In December 2003, it was revealed that on 4 October that year, US and British forces had seized a German-flagged ship in the Mediterranean – the *BBC China* – which was carrying centrifuge parts that could be used to enrich uranium for nuclear bombs. The vessel was heading to Libya from Malaysia. The United States tipped off the German government and after the vessel cleared the Suez Canal it was ordered by the German government to divert to Toronto, Italy where it was detained. The US government argues that the seizure was a major factor in Libya's December 2003 decision to suspend its WMD programmes.[84]

These examples show that:

1. North Korea has been exporting WMD, their delivery systems or related materials to states of proliferation concern; as well as importing WMD-related materials;
2. there are legal limits to interdiction on the high seas;
3. the PSI net may be capturing legal shipments of arms and dual-use materials; and
4. the details of these interdictions and seizures are being kept secret, perhaps to protect intelligence sources and methods, or perhaps to hide any violations of international law or negative publicity for the PSI.

In summary, US-led at-sea interdictions have been ongoing in the western Indian Ocean and the eastern Mediterranean since the beginning of the war in Afghanistan in 2001. Reported interdictions under the PSI, however, have been either of ships in port or those sailing under a PSI member's flag. And they have not been without controversy. Moreover, the one at-sea interdiction – the *So San* – resulted in the determination by the US government that it had no right to hold the ship or its cargo. Based on these examples, the PSI and its interdictions are likely to raise a host of issues.

CHAPTER THREE

Issues and options

Issues

In launching a new multilateral initiative like the PSI, prospective participants might expect the terms defining its operation to be clear and unambiguous. They might also expect their obligations to be uncomplicated and not particularly onerous. This is not the case with PSI. Moreover, the PSI raises a series of formidable international legal issues for its participants, including possible violations of the innocent passage regime, constraints on legal trade, and the undermining of the Law of the Sea and the UN system.

Definitional issues

One cluster of issues concerns the PSI Principles' definitions of terms such as 'delivery systems', 'related materials', 'good cause' and 'reasonably suspected'. The first two terms could include legitimate sales of weapons or dual-use materials.[1] On what basis can a PSI participant prevent a state from acquiring technology or materials that have a legitimate commercial use?[2] And what if both the supplier and the purchaser claim that the goods are for commercial purposes? The last two terms require considerable elaboration as intelligence failures in the 'war on terrorism' have been common. The 1993 detention of the Chinese vessel *Yinhe*, which was suspected of carrying chemical warfare precursors to Iran, is a specific example of faulty intelligence resulting in an unjustified interdiction.[3] There is no standard definition of 'good cause': 'each state will of necessity need to decide for itself whether good cause has been shown, i.e., each state will need to decide for itself whether the information provided by the requesting state warrants acceding to the request'.[4] Of course, there may be political consequences if the requesting state is the United States and the PSI state does not accede to the request for interdiction.

Even more controversial is the question of the targets of interdiction. The definition of 'states or non-state actors of proliferation concern' is any country or entity that the PSI participants say is engaged in proliferation. More specifically, these states are those that 'the PSI participants involved establish should be subject to interdiction activities because they are engaged in proliferation through: (1) efforts to develop or acquire chemical, biological, or nuclear weapons and associated delivery systems; or (2) transfers (either selling, receiving, or facilitating) of WMD, their delivery systems, or related materials'. A state's non-ratification of or non-adherence to non-proliferation treaties or regimes is not adequate basis for considering it a state 'of proliferation concern'.[5] But does this definition apply only to states that do not yet have WMD, or to states that wish to expand their WMD capability, or only to certain of these latter states? For example, North Korea claims to be a nuclear power and is listed by the CIA as such.[6] Israel, India and Pakistan are generally considered to be nuclear powers but remain outside the Nuclear Non-Proliferation Treaty (NPT). South Korea has conducted experiments that could have led to nuclear weapons.[7] What is the legal justification for singling out vessels or aircraft engaged in the 'transfer or transport of WMD, their delivery systems, and related materials' to or from North Korea, and ignoring the same in respect of other nuclear powers? John Bolton has rationalised this double standard by arguing that these non-NPT states are of secondary importance because they do not 'pose the most immediate threat' (to PSI participants).[8]

The interpretation of these definitions and the decision to undertake an interdiction are likely to vary with politics and timing.[9] Thus these decisions will vary from country to country as policymakers consider the political context and consequences. For example, would it be wise for the United States to interdict a North Korean vessel during the fragile Six-Party Talks? Or would Japan be likely to interdict a Chinese vessel in the midst of rising tensions in the East China Sea?

PSI obligations
The PSI places several obligations on its participants. They must 'dedicate appropriate resources and efforts to interdiction operations and capabilities'. They must take specific actions in support of interdiction efforts, including stopping and searching in their internal waters, territorial seas or contiguous

zones vessels that are reasonably suspected of transporting such cargoes. And they must do this at the request and in light of 'good cause' shown by another state, most likely the United States. If the suspicion or cause proves unfounded, the interdicting state would presumably be liable for any cost or damage incurred by the target vessel or aircraft, including to its cargo.[10]

Then there is the matter of the sharing and control of sensitive intelligence. There will have to be a careful trade-off between providing sufficient intelligence to show cause and protecting intelligence methods and sources. The United States is unlikely to trust all PSI participant nations equally with its intelligence and, given past US intelligence failures, these nations may not be willing to act on skimpy or suspect intelligence.

Moreover, the interdicting country will have to decide if the WMD material in the hands of the intended recipient would constitute a significant enough threat to warrant action.[11] They would also want to determine if the intended recipient has a legitimate civilian use for the material. Answers to these questions require clear current intelligence. Further, the intelligence will probably have to pass different thresholds regarding its ability to support a decision for interdiction.[12] These thresholds will likely vary between and even within nations, and with the action intended, e.g., interdiction, boarding, inspection, diversion or seizure.

International law issues
According to Bolton, the PSI 'is without question, legitimate'.[13] This may be true so far: details of PSI interdictions have not been revealed and no country has yet taken the US to the International Tribunal on the Law of the Sea or any other international judicial body. What can be said is that PSI actions certainly test the limits of international law and may eventually exceed them.

Innocent passage. The agreed Principles apply in ports, internal waters, territorial waters and contiguous zones (where declared). But navigation in the territorial waters of any coastal state is subject to the innocent passage regime; that is, it is allowed as long as it is not prejudicial to the coastal state's peace, good order or security.[14] Although specific non-innocent acts are listed in UNCLOS, Article 19, transporting WMD components or missiles are not among them. And Article 23 of UNCLOS explicitly gives ships carrying nuclear weapons the right of innocent passage. Thus, the coastal state would probably have to have legislation in place criminalising WMD proliferation or demonstrate that the vessel is threatening its security because of the presence on board of WMD destined for persons intending to undertake terrorist activities in areas under its jurisdiction,[15] or argue that because the recipient of the WMD is unknown, it has to assume they are bound for an enemy.

Usually the reasons justifying such action include infringements of customs legislation, tax law, immigration or health regulations. If the PSI countries try to use customs legislation to justify such action they will probably have to adjust it to apply specifically to WMD. Nevertheless, it should be possible for countries to develop national laws to interdict aircraft and ships over and in their territorial sea suspected of carrying WMD-related materials.

Legal trade. Parties to the NPT agree not to transfer nuclear weapons or control over such weapons and not to 'assist encourage or induce any non-nuclear weapon state to manufacture or otherwise acquire nuclear weapons'.[16] But it is not illegal for non-signatories to the NPT or the Missile Control Technology Regime (MCTR) to ship nuclear materials or missiles to each other. Nor is it illegal to trade commercially in explosives and conventional arms. There is also the problem of the lack of definitions of nuclear, chemical or biological weapons and, particularly, the term 'related materials'.[17] Some chemical and biological materials have dual uses. The NPT, the Chemical Weapons Convention (CWC) and the Biological and Toxic Weapons Convention (BWC) all expressly provide signatory states with the right to possess and trade dual-use materials.

North Korea is the leading exporter of medium-range ballistic missiles, an important source of its foreign exchange. However, in 2002, the United States was the world's largest exporter of weapons, followed by Russia and France. Some US allies, such as France, Italy and Israel, sell missiles to other countries, as do China and Russia.[18] These items travel by sea.[19] India and China – as well as Serbia, Iran and North Korea – allegedly aided Libya's missile programmes,[20] while Pakistan or its citizens aided both Iran and Libya's nuclear programmes.[21] Israel has modified US-supplied *Harpoon* cruise missiles to carry nuclear warheads that can be launched from submarines.[22] The shipment of such missiles by the United States would seem to violate the PSI Principles. And Japan, in conjunction with the United States, is planning to develop and export missile components to third countries, albeit for 'interceptor' missiles.[23] The point is that if a country like North Korea uses its own properly flagged ships, its arms imports and exports, including nuclear materials or missiles, would be protected by international law in the same way that US and other countries' arms shipments are protected.

In April 2005, the shipment of a German crane to a blacklisted company in Iran supposedly tested the effectiveness of the PSI.[24] The crane was suspected of being used in the manufacture of ballistic missiles. The United States monitored the situation closely. The Norwegian company that chartered the ship was informed that the German government was querying the shipment because of its purchaser and destination. However, there was no request to halt or re-route the vessel, and it apparently reached its destination in Iran with the crane on board.

Undermining the Law of the Sea. PSI interdictions on the high seas would greatly enhance its efficiency, but would also create serious problems. Article 110 of the UNCLOS allows the interdiction and boarding of vessels in EEZs and on the high seas (beyond 12nm from national baselines) only in specific circumstances. These are: if the country under whose flag the ship is sailing gives its permission; if the ship is stateless; if it is a pirate vessel; if it is transporting slaves; or if it is being used for unauthorised broadcasting.[25] An interdiction may be justified by asserting a link between a ship manned by a terrorist organisation and the flag state of the boarding vessel, such as when terrorist acts have been committed in areas under the jurisdiction of the boarding state. One other possibility would involve a situation where hostages are on board the vessel who are nationals of the boarding vessel's flag state.[26] Any other interdiction would violate current international law. Moreover, according to UNCLOS Article 95, on the high seas, warships and government ships used for exclusively non-commercial purposes have complete immunity from the jurisdiction of any other state. This could include government vessels transporting weapons to other states on a non-commercial basis.

Denmark, Turkey and the United States,[27] like North Korea, have not ratified the UNCLOS, but the United States has long maintained that its provisions, particularly those ensuring freedom of navigation on the high seas, are customary international law. Moreover, all of the other countries in the PSI coalition of about 20 have ratified UNCLOS. Thus, high seas interdictions, whether agreed by the PSI group or not, could undermine the carefully nurtured balance enshrined under the UNCLOS. The UNCLOS arose as a 'grand bargain' between coastal developing states and the maritime powers and is seen by most countries as a package deal. A major point of contention during two decades of acrimonious negotiations was the desire of developing coastal states to limit the freedom of navigation and thus the potential for 'gunboat' diplomacy of the maritime powers. However, the maritime powers – led by the United States – insisted on extremely broad freedom of navigation out of concern that extended jurisdiction could hamper their naval and air access and mobility. For example, the United States, the United Kingdom, France and Japan have asserted their right to transport environmentally dangerous nuclear materials through other nations' EEZs.[28] The Bush administration supports ratification of the UNCLOS. But, ironically, the chief domestic opposition to US ratification from neo-conservatives is now primarily because it would enshrine freedom of navigation and thus undermine the PSI.[29] On March 1983, the United States reluctantly proclaimed a 200nm EEZ[30] to stop jurisdictional claims from creeping further seaward or increasing restrictions on freedom of navigation. Now other countries may see it as in their interest to accept the US's PSI to prevent further undermining of freedom of navigation. UNCLOS Article 110 qualifies the general prohibition on high seas boardings by stating, 'except where acts of interference derive from powers conferred by treaty'.[31] Thus, the way to legally exempt interdiction on the high seas from the prohibitions of the UNCLOS is to insert the authority to interdict based on suspicion of transport of WMD-related materials into another treaty. This is why the United States has been trying to amend the 1988 Convention for the Suppression of Unlawful Acts Against the Safety of Maritime Navigation (SUA) to include provisions for interdicting vessels suspected of carrying WMD-related materials.

The PSI also provides for interdiction of aircraft suspected of transporting WMD. Although efforts in this area have progressed more slowly, the United States has stated that it would consider – as a last resort – shooting down any aircraft suspected of transporting WMD and that refuses to land and be searched. The US government would first contact cooperating countries to set up a no-fly zone for a specific plane, and then dispatch military aircraft to intercept it.[32] However, if the aircraft was in international airspace, such action would be highly controversial. The United States has long argued, most recently after the EP-3E incident, when a Chinese fighter and a US surveillance plane collided over China's 200nm Exclusive Economic Zone (EEZ), that aircraft have complete freedom of overflight over the high seas, including EEZs. Moreover, the United States argues that the regime of overflight beyond the territorial sea is governed by the 1944 Chicago International Civil Aviation Convention rather than the UNCLOS. However, in October 1985, US fighter aircraft forced an Egyptian aircraft flying over the Mediterranean and carrying the *Achille Lauro* hijackers from Egypt to Syria, to land in Sicily.[33] This was considered by at least one leading analyst as an illegal act.[34]

As well as deviating from the traditional US staunch defence of freedom of navigation, such 'exceptions' or 'arrangements' being proposed by Washington could over time create new law and practice. Of great concern to some nations is the possibility that the United States or (less likely) members of the PSI coalition might interdict shipments within their waters without their concurrence or knowledge. Indeed, Secretary Rumsfeld has said that the United States would be prepared to mount a maritime interdiction effort anywhere the potential benefits for US security outweigh the costs.

Operating outside the UN system. The question has arisen as to whether the PSI will operate within or outside the UN system. Indeed, some see the PSI as a US attempt to set up multilateral structures outside the UN and other internationally recognised frameworks to project and perpetuate US interests. That may be what is intended.[35] Secretary Rumsfeld has heartily endorsed the PSI as a good example of positive initiatives outside the United Nations or NATO systems because 'one ought not to expect every country to agree with every other country on every single issue all the time'.[36]

Compensation. An issue that will inevitably arise is who is entitled to and liable for compensation for illegal interdictions or interdictions based on faulty intelligence. If the United States interdicted a North Korean-flagged vessel on the high seas and seized its cargo, it would be required to pay reparations.[37] But reparations take into account any contributory wilful or negligent action of the injured state. The United States could argue that trafficking in missiles and WMD involves negligence. If the United States did not claim a legal right to interdict, most states would probably not publicly oppose the action. It could be argued that based on the 'doctrine of necessity' the illegality of the interdiction should be excused by the seriousness of the threat that WMD pose. 'The doctrine of necessity is an international version of the national criminal laws that excuse criminal behaviour caused by distress.'[38] However, using this argument would be a last resort and it could not legally be used repeatedly. Moreover, 'necessity' and imminent peril must be clearly demonstrated.

Dilution of non-proliferation efforts. The PSI is but one tool in a panoply of non-proliferation measures. At a time when the wider non-participation architecture is under severe strain and in need of rejuvenation, the enormous political capital and military effort being expended on the PSI may be weakening efforts in other critical areas, like control of the fuel cycle, expanding to new targets the number of Nunn–Lugar Cooperative Threat Reduction programmes, enhancing export controls and detection technologies, and responding to regional proliferation' hot spots'.[39] The PSI cannot by itself prevent WMD proliferation, although its aggressive promotion by the US may well create the impression that it is the prime non-proliferation tool.

The PSI is plagued by lack of clarity and double standards in its definitions which are linked to potentially onerous obligations of participants. It also raises a series of international legal issues including the possible violation of the innocent passage regime, a negative impact on legal trade, and the undermining of both the Law of the Sea and the UN System. These concerns have created controversy and limited participation in the PSI.

However, there are options for addressing these concerns, although each option has its obstacles and implications.

Options and obstacles
The United States and its 'loose coalition' of PSI partners have several options for increasing PSI participation and enhancing its effectiveness.

Change existing international law
Firstly, the US and its PSI partners could try to change international law to allow such interdictions on and over the high seas. There are apparently discussions underway between Australia, Japan and the United States to do just that.[40] One may argue that a customary law against trafficking in nuclear weapons components has formed, but it is a stretch to claim that such customary law exists regarding trade in missiles. It is another matter altogether to claim the right to interdict shipments on the high seas or perhaps even in innocent passage in the territorial sea.

Ultimately, if enough nations, particularly flag states, outlaw WMD transfers, such interdictions may become acceptable in international law. That is to say, the regime of freedom of the high seas and of innocent passage can be changed by the practice of enough states over time. However, customary law is weaker than treaty law, and such practice could encounter stiff resistance from other maritime powers, and it would run counter to the long-term interests of the United States and those maritime powers that depend on unhindered freedom of navigation. And if a group of nations reached an agreement that runs counter to the UNCLOS, what would be its legal status, and the implications for UNCLOS? Moreover, US attempts to create new legal norms may be undermined by its alleged flaunting of existing ones like the Geneva Conventions regarding its treatment of prisoners in Guantanamo Bay and by its refusal to join the International Criminal Court and the Comprehensive Test Ban Treaty.

A UN resolution or sanctions
The United States may argue that the UN Security Council Presidential Statement of January 1992[41] provides both the political and legal authority for interdicting ships and planes carrying WMD on and over the high seas and in territorial waters. The statement says that the proliferation of all WMD constitutes a threat to international peace and security, and underlines the need for UN member states to prevent WMD proliferation. It may also argue that UN Security Council resolutions (1368, 1373 and 1377)[42] passed in the wake of the 11 September 2001 attacks authorise fighting by

a wide variety of means any terrorist threats to international peace and security, and that their language is broad enough to justify such interdictions on the high seas.[43]

But use of these general statements in such a way would be highly controversial and require clarification. Thus, in March 2004, the United States and the United Kingdom began an effort to obtain a UN Security Council Resolution specifically authorising states to interdict, board and inspect any vessel or aircraft if there is reason to believe it is carrying WMD or the technology to make or deliver them, and to seize or impound missiles, related technology or equipment. This was a difficult tacit admission by the United States that it needs a UN mandate to legitimise high seas PSI interdictions. It was also hoped that such a resolution would also prohibit UN member states from purchasing, receiving, assisting or allowing the transfer of missile or missile-related equipment and technology from specified states.[44] Monitoring trade in WMD would also probably require a subcommittee and a small secretariat.

Chinese and Russian opposition to the UNSC resolution authorising the invasion of Iraq made passage of a resolution including high seas interdiction very unlikely. Indeed, as it turned out, the potential vetoes of China or Russia posed particularly formidable obstacles. The United States might have instead tried to use the Uniting for Peace Resolution[45] in the UN General Assembly to obtain legal justification for interdicting ships on the high seas or those of a particular country, for example, North Korea. But this would require a two-thirds majority, which would have been very difficult to obtain.[46] Nevertheless, some observers thought such a resolution might be acceptable because of the increasing recognition that the spread of WMDs is a threat to world peace, and provided the United States was willing to negotiate and compromise. This was possible with the Safety of Life at Sea (SOLAS) amendments and the new International Maritime Organisation (IMO) security code.[47]

There were several initial objections to the draft introduced to the UNSC. Foremost was the question of what constitutes 'WMD-related materials'. Another particular area of debate was the text's proposal that parties 'to the extent consistent with their national legal authorities and international law' cooperate in preventing, and if necessary interdicting, shipments of WMD and related materials. Also subject to debate was the draft's requirement that states report their compliance to the President of the Security Council regarding their national laws and support for strengthening multilateral treaties. Further, the text did not include a British proposal for a UN counter-proliferation committee, or a French proposal for a permanent corps of UN weapons inspectors. In other words, according to the US proposal, enforcement would be outside the UN system but legitimised by it.

After considerable debate in and outside the Security Council, a revised draft resolution emerged which asked all UN members to 'criminalise' the proliferation of WMD, enact strict export controls and secure all sensitive materials within their own borders.[48] The idea was that if more countries criminalised WMD exports, the coalition would have more legal basis to interdict them.

The final resolution, introduced to the Security Council on 24 March 2004 and passed on 28 April 2004 (UNSCR 1540) requires the UN's 191 members to 'adopt and enforce appropriate effective laws to prevent any non-state actor from being able to manufacture, acquire, possess, develop, transport or use nuclear, chemical or biological weapons and their means of delivery'.[49] Specifically, it compels all countries to adopt laws to criminalise the spread of WMD, to ensure that they have strong export controls and to secure sensitive materials within their borders.[50]

Russia and China prevented a specific endorsement of interdiction and the PSI in the final Resolution.[51] However, the United States argues that Paragraph 10 essentially authorises it.[52] That paragraph calls upon 'all states – in accordance with their national legal authorities and legislation and consistent with international law – to take cooperative action to step, impede, intercept and otherwise prevent the illicit trafficking in these weapons, their means of delivery and related materials'.[53] This text was agreed only after the United States accepted China's demand (under a threat of a veto) to drop a provision specifically authorising the interdiction of vessels suspected of transporting WMD, a cornerstone of the PSI. China also objected to any suggestion that the Council endorse *ad hoc* frameworks like PSI. But Bolton claimed that China's representative acknowledged that 'cooperative action to prevent illicit trafficking' would cover the interdiction of ships carrying WMD, by arguing in private that the word 'interdict' is redundant. Nevertheless, it is not clear if the Chinese government agrees with this interpretation.

With these amendments, China, France and Russia supported the revised draft. However, a vote was delayed because Council members wanted all 191 UN member states to be briefed on the Resolution.[54] Ironically, Pakistan, a prominent US ally in the war on terrorism, led opposition to the Resolution[55] until it was assured it would not be retroactive and a provision allowing intrusive inspections was deleted. Opponents of the Resolution were also concerned by the Security Council's assumption of the authority to essentially make national law, and possible sanctions against UN members who did not comply. They also objected to the secrecy with which the text was negotiated among only the Permanent Five before its introduction. The Resolution has done little to strengthen the effectiveness of PSI since it focuses only on non-state actors and does not clearly authorise interdiction, or any action outside current international law.

Nevertheless, some may argue that by requiring states to prohibit the transfer of WMD, their means of delivery and related materials, the Resolution authorises the interdiction on the high seas of such shipments – at least to non-state groups.[56] Indicating that the United States may try to use this rationale, the US State Department's Bureau of Non-Proliferation web page quotes paragraph 10 of UNSCR 1540 which 'calls upon all states to take cooperative action to stop, impede, intercept and otherwise prevent the illicit trafficking in nuclear, chemical or biological weapons, their means of delivery and related materials' to justify the PSI.[57] However, it adds the qualifier 'in accordance with their national legal authorities and legislation and consistent with international law', and also publicly states that 'if a state believes it does not have the legal authorities to act in a specific action, it may decline to participate'.[58] Thus it is unclear if the United States thinks UNSCR 1540 provides authority for high seas interdictions, and in any event it theoretically allows a PSI state to disagree that it does so.

Although there are no sanctions or enforcement measures if states do not comply with UNSCR 1540, a Security Council Committee will monitor implementation of the Resolution and governments are required to file reports on their efforts to comply, that is, strengthen their domestic laws, and export and border controls.[59] However as of late April 2005, some 75 states had not submitted their first reports to the Committee despite a 28 October 2004 deadline. This indicates both administrative difficulties and a lack of concern by some states.[60] Since the Resolution was adopted under Chapter III of the UN Charter, in theory the use of force or sanctions could follow. Nevertheless, at best, this Resolution would tighten international treaties and domestic safeguards, but not break new ground. Moreover it is not easy for governments to stop such shipments. For example, the Humayun Khan network (not the A.Q. Khan network) illegally exported from the United States to Pakistan specialised equipment that can be used to test, develop and detonate nuclear weapons.[61] These shipments were routed through South Africa to avoid suspicion.

Without a clearly worded Resolution specifically authorising high seas interdiction, any such interdictions over the objection of the flag state would be tantamount to aggression and could be considered an act of war. And even if each PSI country were to enforce the PSI Principles only in its own territorial waters, each interdiction may require Security Council approval,[62] or only be applicable in very specific circumstances.

United Nations Secretary-General Kofi Annan supports the PSI.[63] But he would prefer that such issues and actions be addressed and undertaken collectively through and by the United Nations.[64] He has said that the Security Council must be 'the sole source of legitimacy on the use of force'.[65] French President Jacques Chirac also favours this approach, proposing a Security Council summit meeting to frame a UN action plan against proliferation and creating a corps of inspectors to carry it out. However, in 2005 there is a growing sense in the Bush administration and other PSI countries that current weapons-control regimes and the United Nations system itself are not working well enough or fast enough to suit their needs.[66] Indeed, Bolton has argued that Annan's insistence on the Security Council being the sole source of legitimacy in the use of force is 'unsupported by over 50 years of experience with the UN Charter's operation', referring in particular to the non-UN-sanctioned US/NATO intervention in Kosovo in 1999.[67] More recently, US Secretary of State Condoleezza Rice has stated that the PSI provides an effective way to deal with North Korean attempts to trade in WMD and that it does not need or require Security Council authorisation.[68]

Another possibility would be for the UN to issue sanctions against a particular proliferating country like Iran or North Korea. The Bush administration is reportedly contemplating seeking a UNSC resolution to this effect.[69] Such sanctions or a resolution could be used to justify seizures. Or, interdictions might be undertaken even because of the *suspicion* of a violation, followed by a search for illicit materials. But these options would likely encounter the same obstacles reviewed above, including opposition from China. They may even be quietly opposed by Japan and South Korea out of concern with antagonising North Korea and thus being an initial target of its wrath.[70] Nevertheless, like UNSC Resolution 1441, which the United States used to justify the invasion of Iraq, the authorisation could provide some legal rationale for interdictions. Interdictions under such authorisation, though, would be controversial and unlikely to engender wide international cooperation or support.[71]

Develop a new convention or amend the 1982 UNCLOS
The PSI coalition could develop a new convention on weapons proliferation or an amendment to the UNCLOS. However, the so-called 'rogue' states would not ratify such a measure and thus not be bound by it. Thus, such a convention would only be useful if the shipments of WMD,

related materials or their delivery systems entered the territorial waters or airspace of signatories. Nevertheless, legislation is already pending in the US Congress – the Missile Threat Reduction Act of 2003 – which calls for a US-led effort to seek a binding international instrument to restrict the trade of offensive missiles.[72]

Regarding an amendment to the UNCLOS, under Article 312 a state party can propose specific amendments and request the convening of a conference to consider them. If more than half of the state parties approve within a year, a conference will be convened. However, the United States has not ratified the Convention and thus can neither propose nor officially oppose any amendments.[73] Indeed, one of the reasons the US Homeland Security Department and the Department of Defense support US ratification of the treaty is that it would enhance the US ability to conduct interdiction operations.[74]

Declare that WMD shipments are not a peaceful use of the oceans
Article 88 of UNCLOS states that 'the high seas shall be reserved for peaceful purposes'.[75] The United States and its allies might assert that sea trade in WMD and related materials is not peaceful, and thus such ships can be seized. But who has the authority to stop such shipments – any state, any groups of states authorised by the UN, or the states whose peace is potentially threatened? The use of this provision would be very difficult for the United States. Firstly, it has not ratified the Convention. More importantly, when China has used this provision to protest US military and intelligence gathering activities in its EEZ, arguing that it constitutes a threat to its security, the United States has argued that these activities are defensive and thus 'peaceful'.[76]

Strengthen SUA
The 1985 terrorist hijacking of the passenger liner *Achille Lauro* indirectly led to the International Maritime Organization (IMO) sponsorship of the 1988 Rome conference from which emerged support for a Convention for the Suppression of Unlawful Acts Against the Safety of Maritime Navigation Convention (SUA).[77] SUA was meant to: 'fill many of the jurisdictional gaps highlighted when the acts endanger the safety of international navigation and occur on board national or foreign flag ships while underway in the territorial sea, international straits or international waters. The Convention requires state parties to criminalize such acts under national law and to cooperate in the investigation and prosecution of their perpetrators.'[78] As of March 2003, the SUA had been ratified by 95 states representing more than 76% of world merchant shipping. Although the Convention

was developed in large part in response to the *Achille Lauro* incident and with the objective of combating terrorism, it can also be an anti-piracy and anti-sea robbery measure.[79] Indeed, if a person seizes control of a ship by force, or threat thereof, or performs an act of violence likely to endanger the ship's safe navigation, the person has committed an offence under the Convention, regardless of the motive.

In 2002, the United States proposed amendments to SUA that would add new offences to Article 3 and Article 2 of the SUA Protocol, including the presence of tools or substances useful in WMD and the use of the ship for transport of such substances, and which would allow boarding of a suspect vessel without permission of the flag state if no response is received within four hours.[80] The UK has supported these proposed amendments[81] from the beginning and Japan now supports them as well.[82] Although the IMO Legal Committee recognises the need to address offences that threaten state security, these specific proposals have not been well received by other state parties to the IMO.[83] Reservations regarding the draft included concern that it could jeopardise the principle of freedom of navigation and other established international laws, that the IMO is not the competent forum for dealing with non-proliferation issues, and that the SUA Convention is not the appropriate instrument.[84] There are also specific serious concerns with the definitions of prohibited items, the provisions for boarding, and the evidence required for boarding including the motive and prior knowledge of the transporter, as well as human-rights concerns. These reservations were again expressed at the 88th session of the IMO Legal Committee on 19–23 April 2004.[85] The Legal Committee has tried ardently to reach agreement on the language to be used[86] and the drafts are now ready for consideration.[87] A conference of state parties will be held in London in October 2005 to adopt amendments to the Treaty. But even if the provisions are eventually endorsed by the state parties to SUA, it would not prevent such shipments on a non-state party's own flagged vessels.

Obtain NATO endorsement

Another possibility is for NATO to integrate its intelligence and capabilities with the PSI.[88] According to the UN Charter, regional security organisations such as NATO are permitted to take measures to 'secure' their regions, which for NATO includes most of Europe and North America. Since WMD pose a potential threat to global security, NATO could claim broad authority to interdict weapons and their enabling material destined for 'rogue' states. The Bush administration could face challenges in winning NATO's support for such action, as all of its members must agree in principle for it to receive alliance approval. Nevertheless, the United States believes all of NATO's members can be brought on board.[89] However, the UN Charter does not explicitly allow regional organisations to act in the place of the Security Council.[90] Moreover, although NATO has an institutional incentive to add new missions to legitimise its post-Cold War function, the 'out of area' concept remains controversial.[91] Additionally, countries critical to the effectiveness of the PSI such as China and Russia are not NATO members.

Reinterpret, or rewrite and expand adherence to, the NPT
Another avenue is for the United States to pressure more countries to join the NPT and the International Atomic Energy Agency's (IAEA) Additional Protocol and to make their provisions less ambiguous.[92] The Additional Protocol strengthens the IAEA's investigative power 'to verify compliance with NPT safeguard obligations and provides the IAEA with the ability to act quickly, including surprise inspections, regarding any indications of undeclared nuclear materials, facilities and activities'.[93] The idea of this particular approach is to establish a set of 'triggers' that would identify a country as a nuclear risk, as well as to prescribe the international response the triggers would require. However, this would be politically difficult.[94]

The United States already interprets the NPT as obligating members to interdict vessels suspected of carrying illegal nuclear materials in their territorial waters, although the NPT Treaty is not explicit in this regard. Article I provides that state parties to the Treaty undertake not to transfer nuclear weapons or nuclear explosive devices, or control over such materials directly or indirectly, and not to assist any non-nuclear weapon state in acquiring or controlling them.[95] Perhaps the US can argue that this includes not allowing their passage through their territorial waters. However, this is not clear, and if it does prohibit such passage, there may be a legal clash with the regime of innocent passage.

Two of the countries of proliferation concern, Syria and Iran, are parties to the NPT and have standard safeguard agreements with the IAEA. Iran has also signed the Additional Protocol,[96] but Syria has not done so.[97] Syria has received assistance from North Korea – which withdrew from the NPT in January 2003 – and non-government Iranian entities in its ballistic missile development. Convincing Syria to sign the Additional Protocol is somewhat difficult for the United States because Israel is not a party to the NPT, although it is widely considered to have nuclear weapons.[98] Moreover, the new US effort to develop small, low-yield nuclear weapons may not only be considered nuclear proliferation by some, but may prompt others to develop similar weapons.[99]

In May 2005, at the NPT Review Conference in New York, the United States proposed that the NPT be amended to clarify and incorporate UN Security Council Resolution 1540 to prevent illicit trading in nuclear materials and technology and urged adherents to support the PSI.[100] However, at this time, some nuclear states did not participate in the Conference or choose to be bound by modification of the NPT, e.g., North Korea, Israel, India and Pakistan. Moreover, the US proposal was weakened by its opposition to provisions for inspections and verification in a new treaty that would have banned production of nuclear weapons materials, thus reinforcing the NPT.[101] The official reason for the US reluctance to agree to the new treaty was that verification would have been too intrusive and difficult and thus few countries would accept it. But proponents of the treaty argued that without verification the treaty would be weak, and it would be harder to prevent nuclear materials from reaching terrorists. Washington's proposals were also undermined by the US failure to divest itself of its stockpile of nuclear weapons, as required by the NPT, and indications that it is even considering developing new tactical nuclear weapons. It has even been alleged that the United States and other acknowledged nuclear powers 'routinely' violate the NPT.[102] The Canadian representative to the NPT Review Conference, Paul Meyer, apparently referring to the Bush administration, said at the close of the Conference, 'if governments simply ignore or discard commitments whenever they prove inconvenient, we will never be able to build an edifice of international cooperation'.[103] According to one critic, 'in the course of the four-week meeting of representatives of the 188 countries which have signed and ratified the treaty, the United States refused to uphold its previous arms control pledges, blocked consideration of the establishment of a nuclear-free zone in the Middle East, refused to rule out US nuclear attacks against non-nuclear states, and demanded that Iran and North Korea – but not US allies like Israel – be singled out for UN sanctions for their nuclear programs'.[104] The NPT Review Conference ended in abject failure.[105] However, *ad hoc* agreements among states that close loopholes in the existing treaty remain an option.

Argue self-defence

The concept of pre-emptive self-defence includes anticipatory self-defence and preventive self-defence.[106] The United States and its coalition partners might invoke Article 51 of the United Nations Charter arguing that in the wake of the attacks of 11 September 2001, WMD in the hands of their *avowed enemies* constitute a clear and imminent threat to their security, and that they are entitled to anticipatory self-defence. Or they could argue that the 'inherent right' to self-defence in Article 51 signifies a retention of the right of self-defence under pre-charter customary law. Regarding North Korea, the United States could argue that it has threatened to export pluto-nium, and has a history of exporting arms to 'rogue' states.

Indeed, the United States believes it already has the legal authority for such interdictions.[107] For example, Bolton has argued that self-defence justi-fies interdicting North Korea ships carrying WMD, their delivery systems and related materials.[108] And the White House has stated that '[the United States] will not hesitate to act alone, if necessary, to exercise our right of self-defence by acting pre-emptively against such terrorists, to prevent them from doing harm against our people and our country'.[109] Thus the Bush administration's own test for pre-emptive self-defence appears to be a 'specific threat to the United States or [its] allies and friends'.[110]

The US military is considering allowing regional commanders to request presidential approval for pre-emptive nuclear strikes against possible attacks with WMD on the United States or its allies.[111] And President Bush has nominated two maritime leaders – Marine General Peter Pace and Navy Admiral Edmund Giambastiani – as Chairman and Vice Chairman of the Joint Chiefs of Staff.[112] This may indicate that the maritime arena will receive greater emphasis in future military planning.

However, for an action to be compatible with present international legal interpretations of anticipatory self-defence, the United States and its coalition partners would probably not only have to demonstrate that the interdicted cargo required interdiction because it posed a specific and imminent threat of attack on the United States or its allies, but that the necessity of self-defence was instant and overwhelming, leaving no choice of means, and no time for deliberation.[113] That is, a response was necessary, proportional to the threat and the threat was imminent.[114] Otherwise such action and argument would greatly expand the traditional definition of self-defence to include pre-emptive self-defence regarding non-imminent threats, and would set a very dangerous precedent that could under-mine the foundations of the United Nations. Strictly interpreted, article 51 provides the right of self-defence only in the case of an armed attack and only until the UN 'Security Council has taken measures necessary to maintain international peace and security'.[115]

Nevertheless, the December 2004 report of the UN Secretary General's High Level Panel on Threats, Challenges and Change suggests broaden-ing 'the interpretation [of article 51] to allow the preventive use of force in some instances, but only if approved by the UN Security Council'.[116] The Security Council would judge the legitimacy of such action by 'whether it met the age-old criteria of a just war: the seriousness of the threat, the purpose of the response, whether force is a last resort, whether it is used in a proportionate way, and whether there is a reasonable balance of good and bad consequences'.[117] The Panel concluded that preventive force can be justified, but not its unilateral use. Secretary-General Annan has recommended the Security Council adopt 'a set of clear principles' governing the use of pre-emptive force.[118] Significantly, the same Panel report, as well as Annan, also encouraged 'all states to join the PSI'.

Thus, there seems to be a trend towards expanding the meaning of pre-emptive self-defence. If the United States were to interdict, without permission, a vessel on the high seas and claimed pre-emptive self-defence consistent with the PSI, this would create a serious dilemma for other PSI members.[119] They could either acquiesce to this legal claim or publicly protest, thus risking the benefits of the PSI and good relations with the United States. Restricting the proliferation of WMD and reducing the risk of illegal unilateral US action are increasingly incompatible goals.

Continue current efforts to expand the PSI coalition and its supporters
US counter-proliferation goals may be best served by expanding upon existing efforts, including enhanced cooperation in surveillance, intelligence gathering and intelligence exchange. Without amending either national laws or freedom of navigation under the UNCLOS, this would entail relying upon those states willing to cooperate, and waiting until suspect vessels or aircraft enter their territorial waters or airspace, before seizing or forcing them down. An adjunct would be to focus on strengthening screening in ports to prevent such shipments from reaching the high seas.[120] This crackdown could be accompanied by the seizing of proliferators' finances and suspension of their trading licences.[121] In addition, PSI members could seek the support through bilateral agreements of 'flag of convenience' nations, like Costa Rica, Honduras and Cambodia, whose 'flag' vessels are thought to be owned or used by 'terrorists'.[122]

Options for increasing PSI participation and enhancing its effectiveness include changing existing international law; expanding existing conventions or developing a new one; obtaining an unambiguous empowering UN Security Council Resolution; obtaining NATO endorsement; arguing pre-emptive self-defence; and building a coalition of countries willing to perform such interdictions on each other's ships and aircraft in or over their territorial seas. However, each of these options would face obstacles and limitations. The PSI has some way to go before it becomes the widely supported and effective tool its founders envisioned. In sum, it requires a sounder rationale and a longer-term vision.

CHAPTER FOUR

PSI politics and the way forward

US rationale and longer-term strategy

The United States appears to be developing, in an *ad hoc* manner, a long-term strategy to prevent trade in WMD components and related materials. The strategic rationale for the PSI is multifaceted and targets both terrorist challenges by non-state actors and states 'of proliferation concern'. It is built upon many assumptions and perceptions. Firstly, the United States bases its policies on the fundamental principle that preventing a WMD attack by an enemy state or a 'terrorist' group is vital to its national security. Secondly, the US feels its defence must be pre-emptive or even 'preventive' to forestall terrorist attacks such as those on the USS *Cole* and the French tanker *Limburg* in Yemeni waters, as well as those purportedly planned by al-Qaeda operatives against a US ship in Malaysian or Indonesian ports,[1] and against US and UK navy ships in the Straits of Gibraltar.[2] The Bush administration's National Strategy to Combat Weapons of Mass Destruction, issued only days after the *So San* debacle of 12 December 2003, states 'US military forces and appropriate civilian agencies must have the capability to defend against WMD-armed adversaries, including appropriate cases through pre-emptive action'.[3] Further, since the events of 11 September 2001, both President Bush and Vice-President Dick Cheney believe that some terrorist challenges must be met with direct military action,[4] and the PSI can be seen as a statement of intent in that regard. Thirdly, the United States assumes that North Korea has a highly enriched uranium programme, which means that it needs to purchase many components and supplies abroad, implying numerous shipments of these components to North Korea via air, land and sea.[5]

Fourthly, the United States apparently perceives interdiction at sea to be preferable to an embargo to contain North Korean trade in WMD and missiles, curtailing its financial lifeline. It believes an embargo or blockade would be ineffective, particularly if China and South Korea do not participate. Moreover, it believes either would almost certainly trigger war with North Korea, whereas interdiction operations may not do so. The PSI is a middle ground between continuing diplomatic frustration and failure, and all-out military force. If the Six-Party Talks make little or no progress, the United States is likely to step up PSI activities aimed at North Korea.[6]

Fifth, the United States believes that the existing web of export control laws and treaties designed to end the black market in WMD has failed to do so, making the PSI a vital deterrent to WMD traders, or at least to make the trade more difficult, physically and politically, and thus less profitable,[7] therefore putting stress on these countries' economies, particularly that of North Korea. And if North Korea and Iran – like India, Israel and Pakistan – do 'get away' with having nuclear weapons, the PSI can at least be used to stop them from enabling further proliferation.

And sixth, through stepped up US intelligence cooperation, the initiative can serve to identify those vessels and aircraft requiring closer scrutiny. According to then Undersecretary of State for Arms Control and International Security John Bolton, the long-term objective of the PSI is to 'create a web of counter-proliferation partnerships that will impede trade in WMD, delivery systems, and related materials'.[8]

The longer-term US strategy seems to be to expand greatly the loose coalition of countries adhering to the PSI principles until it encompasses most of the world's major flag, port, coastal and transit countries, particularly those that have been used in the past by WMD proliferators (as defined by the United States). It would seem that the plan is to change international law through state practice, that is, the actions of powerful states over a period of time they deem sufficient to claim it is customary international law.[9]

In March 2004, it was announced that the United States and Liberia – a flag of convenience state – had reached an agreement to allow US authorities to board and search for WMD in national and international waters the more than 2,000 commercial ships with Liberian registry.[10] This was a major step forward in the PSI effort. In each case, there must be consultation with Liberia and its consent obtained prior to any boarding. Nevertheless, under the agreement, the United States needs to wait only two hours for a response and no reply is considered approval for boarding.[11] A similar agreement was reached on 12 May 2004 with Panama, the world's number one registry with more than 10,000 vessels under its flag.[12] The agreement was reached after the United States 'claimed Panama was failing to ensure that its flagged ships were complying with new anti-terrorism measures'.[13] This meant that Panamanian-flagged vessels could have been barred from US and European ports if they failed to meet the new requirements by 1 July 2004. This would have destroyed Panama's maritime industry, its major source of income. Panamanian-flagged vessels were already considered suspect because of the country's low standards of shipping safety and security. The US has struck similar agreements with the Republic of the Marshal Islands, Cyprus (April 2005),[14] Croatia (June 2005) and Belize (August 2005).[15] Including PSI participants' ships, this brings to about 60% by dead weight tonnage the portion of the world's shipping fleet that is subject to rapid consent procedures for boarding, search and seizure on the high seas. The United Kingdom also plans to try to negotiate such agreements with the main commercial flag states.[16] Bolton has said that the next goal is to 'reach agreements with nations to deny overflight rights to aircraft suspected of carrying WMD and related materials'.[17]

The corollary to this strategy is to persuade and help countries to change or create national laws that will authorise them to interdict suspicious ships and aircraft and to seize any WMD cargoes in or over their territory, their territorial waters and possibly their contiguous zones as well. An adjunct to this effort would be to establish a very accurate real-time picture of what is travelling by sea – something like a maritime NORAD (North American Aerospace Defense Command – the US-Canadian military command responsible for North American air defences). This system would be similar to air-traffic control systems and involve the knowledge and tracking of shipments from port to port, that is, what is being shipped from where, to where, by whom, along what route.

Such a system is being formulated – Maritime Domain Awareness (MDA). In December 2004, President Bush issued a directive calling for a 'national maritime security blueprint that would co-ordinate efforts of government agencies and the shipping industry to secure containers, protect ports and conduct surveillance over US waters'.[18] It is not clear yet whether NORAD would be expanded to include maritime security or whether it will be treated separately. Maritime surveillance is a key issue in renegotiation of the US–Canada security agreement set to expire in May 2006. A 'Maritime Concept of Operations' was sent to Secretary Rumsfeld in January 2005. This apparently includes a Global Maritime Intelligence

Center integrating the intelligence assets of the Department of Defense, the Department of Homeland Security and other agencies 'to support global maritime surveillance, global maritime interception operations and maritime homeland protection'.[19]

The Bush administration has also agreed to set up a National Counterproliferation Center to be headed by Kenneth Brill, considered by some analysts to have reservations about the PSI.[20] The Center will coordinate US government efforts to stop proliferation of WMD and related materials. The US State Department has created a Bureau for International Security and Nonproliferation by merging the Arms Control and Nonproliferation bureaux. This Bureau will lead control and non-proliferation initiatives and negotiations, focus on the link between WMD and terrorism, and be the principal focal point for promoting the PSI and related non-proliferation efforts.[21] The administration has also promulgated a 'WMD Proliferation Financing Executive Order' that would freeze the US assets of *anyone or any organisation* doing business with WMD proliferators.[22] Its implementation may be more controversial than that of the PSI. Although the directive targets Syrian, North Korean and Iranian entities, not a single Chinese entity was included despite the fact that 62 of the Bush administration's announced proliferation sanctions have been imposed on Chinese entities.[23]

To sum up, the current direction of the PSI is to strengthen cooperation among existing members; expand active participation, particularly to key countries like India and China; forge a web of bilateral boarding agreements and expand SUA; strengthen the process of exercises and discussions; expand the operational environment from maritime to air and ground operations; and build and implement an MDA system.[24] Despite the development of this multi-pronged strategy, PSI effectiveness continues to be limited by the lack of participation of key countries and even the full participation of some publicly declared participants. Each has its own political calculus to consider.

PSI-related political issues

Unlike the unilateral US 'quarantine' against the island nation of Cuba, the PSI on a practical political level requires the cooperation of many other countries, including North Korea's neighbours. But key countries in Northeast Asia have not yet participated in the PSI and may not do so. China, and even more notably South Korea have so far declined to participate, although they are being pressured to do so by the US.[25] Even Japan, which has agreed to the PSI Principles, is unclear as to the depth and breadth of its participation,[26] partly because of its concern about provoking North Korea. Pyongyang has repeatedly said it would view an embargo or interdictions as an act of war that would abrogate the 27 July 1953 Armistice Agreement, which ended the Korean War.[27] These key countries fear that the stronger the PSI pressure – i.e., the likelier the prospects of interdiction of North Korean vessels – the stronger the reaction will be from North Korea. Confirming North Korea's fears, during the October 2004 PSI exercise hosted by Japan, Bolton pointedly said that the exercise should send a message to North Korea. But if these key Northeast Asian countries do not participate, the interdiction 'net' could have fatal holes.

Japan has taken pains to emphasise that the PSI does not specifically target North Korea, and it is unclear if Japan has committed to interdicting North Korea vessels. The use of Japanese warships on the high seas for such interdictions could raise sensitive issues for Japan both domestically and among its neighbours who suffered from Japanese aggression in the Second World War. Indeed, the involvement of Japan's navy (the Maritime Self-Defense Force, JMSDF) in the PSI around Japan would produce strong objections from North Korea, China and probably South Korea. Moreover, under Japanese law, its naval and coast guard vessels can only intercept ships flying the Japanese flag. For example, under Japanese laws, JMSDF destroyers which are currently in the Persian Gulf to support US operations in Iraq can only guard a neighbouring area if a JMSDF supply ship is refuelling foreign vessels,[28] and warships from other countries can not guard JMSDF ships because that would be collective self-defence which is constitutionally prohibited[29] because it exceeds 'the minimum necessary level of self-defence'.[30]

Until June 2004, Japan remained one of the few nations that has no domestic legal basis to board suspicious vessels on the high seas with flag-state consent.[31] However, in a significant departure from the status quo, in April 2002, laws introduced by the government enable the JMSDF 'to inspect without their consent ships on the high seas close to Japan if Japan believes they are headed for a country which has attacked or is on the verge of attacking Japan'.[32] The previous law allowed JMSDF actions only in emergencies to maintain public peace and order, or to carry out inspections based on UN Security Council resolutions or with the consent of the flag state, and no warning shots were permitted in either case. The new law allows the JMSDF to fire warning shots even at privately owned boats, and to confiscate cargos of arms, ammunition or WMD. In June 2004, the Japanese parliament passed the Emergency Legislation to Deal with Military Attacks from Abroad,[33] enabling the JMSDF to control the operation of ships in Japanese territorial waters or on the high seas close to Japan if it believes they are a threat to Japan.[34] However, this control would only be operative when Japan was under attack, not if it simply anticipates an attack. China views the legislation as a shift in Japan's military strategy from 'defensive' to 'offensive'.[35]

Japan has also created two special units in the JMSDF and the coast guard to respond to intrusions by 'spy ships'.[36] Japan is also training officials from ASEAN countries in the detection and interdiction of WMD and ballistic missiles at sea. Indeed, Japan is taking the lead in trying to gain the support of ASEAN for the PSI, perhaps in part to divert US pressure and attention from its own half-hearted participation.

Japan is under considerable US pressure to become involved in PSI interdictions.[37] The Japanese Defense Agency's Advisory Group for Security and Defense Capabilities advised Prime Minister Junichiro Koizumi in a 4 October 2004 report that WMD were a serious security threat to Japan and that Japan should work with the international community, including the PSI, to prevent their proliferation.[38] Nevertheless, Tokyo postponed its hosting of a PSI exercise scheduled for May 2004 because of its concern with North Korea and because China and South Korea were not supportive. There was disagreement between the Japan Defense Agency (JDA) and the Ministry of Foreign Affairs (MOFA) on the role of JMSDF in the exercise.[39] MOFA views the PSI within the framework of export control while the JDA sees it as part of national security. The Japanese government has strengthened the domestic export control system and has blocked several illegal exports of dual-use materials to North Korea, including missile-related goods originating in Thailand on 8 April 2003 and large tractors originating in China on 30 April 2003.[40]

Japan eventually agreed to host the exercise in late October 2004. Vessels and aircraft from Australia, the United States and other core PSI participants were involved. Out of respect for its neighbours' sensitivities, the targets were a Japanese- and an American-flagged vessel, and the role of the JMSDF was limited to surveillance.[41] Nevertheless, China and South Korea refused even to send observers, and North Korea denounced the exercise as a dangerous provocation. Some Japanese analysts consider a North Korean May 2005 missile test as a warning to Japan against potentially participating in a maritime blockade against North Korea.[42]

So far, Japan's participation in PSI has been low-key in large part due to the MOFA's reluctance to support the commitment of JMSDF assets to the endeavour. However, the PSI was enshrined as a particular area of US–

Japan security cooperation in the 19 February 2005 Joint US–Japan Security Committee Statement.[43] The US and Japanese governments are negotiating a joint role-sharing document that will include strengthening Japan's role in the PSI.[44] Moreover, Japan's MSDF participated in a Singapore-hosted PSI exercise in August 2005 in the South China Sea with 340 armed personnel, the destroyer *Shirane*, two P-3C patrol planes and an airborne warning-and-command system.[45] This is the first time the SDF has sent armed personnel to take part in a PSI exercise overseas and is part of the Japan Defense Agency's plan to have Japan's military forces engage in more joint activities abroad. Nevertheless there was some domestic concern that Japan's active participation in this sensitive area could provoke protests from Indonesia and Malaysia.[46]

Until June 2004, Russia was the only member of the Group of Eight (G-8) industrial nations that was still not a member of the PSI, and was being heavily pressed by the United States to join.[47] Russia was concerned that the PSI in general and the exercises in particular would increase tension and even lead to regional conflict in the Asian region.[48] Moreover, it worried that searches of ships on the open ocean 'could jeopardize international trade, undermine international law and set a bad precedent'.[49] Eventually, after much stalling, in June 2004 Moscow announced it would join PSI, although with the caveat that it would contribute only as long as PSI actions did not violate international law or Russia's own domestic legislation.[50] In practice, Moscow has been less finicky. In January 2005 it was reported that Russia tried to block North Korean exports of missiles through its territory to Iran but failed to do so – perhaps because its interdiction plans were leaked to the smugglers.[51] Russia's implementation of the PSI against Iran is complicated, since Moscow sells weapons to Tehran and is assisting in the construction of a nuclear energy facility at Bushehr, despite the concerns of the International Atomic Energy Agency.[52]

South Korea will probably not join the PSI. Indeed, doing so would be inconsistent with Seoul's fundamental policies.[53] It is concerned about the potential reactions of North Korea and China, as well as the effect on the Six Party Talks. In October 2003, South Korean Unification Minister Jeong Se Hyen requested the United States to take a more conciliatory approach.[54] Nevertheless, the United States continues to press South Korea to join the PSI, including in a May 2005 visit to Seoul by US Assistant Secretary of State for East Asian and Pacific Affairs Christopher Hill. While 'fully understanding the goals of PSI', Minister of Foreign Affairs and Trade Ban Ki Moon reiterated that South Korea must be cautious considering the peculiar situation of the two Koreas'.[55] The US need for South Korea to join the PSI is based primarily on its critical geographic location but also because US interdiction forces may need to operate from South Korean territory. Also, South Korea is North Korea's largest trading partner and allows North Korea to use its territorial waters for through traffic.[56]

Beijing's support for the PSI is considered critical to its success because China controls some of the sealanes leading to North Korea, including the Taiwan Strait, and North Korea has apparently used Chinese airspace to fly shipments of missiles and arms to Iran.[57] Moreover, the United States alleges that North Korean companies in China have purchased chemicals for reprocessing plutonium and for its chemical weapons programmes, and that China helped Pakistan build an unsafeguarded nuclear reactor and provided equipment and know-how for Iran's alleged nuclear programme, as well as designs for a cruise missile. So far, China has not joined or participated in the PSI but is under increasing US pressure to do so. Bolton complained publicly that 'China's government has not done enough to halt arms and missile proliferation to rogue states' and 'that it has ignored US appeals to help stop Chinese companies from transferring arms' to US enemies like Iran.[58] Yet China has stopped some dual-use chemicals from leaving China for North Korea.[59] On the other hand, China intends to import uranium from Australia, a member of the PSI 'coalition'.[60] China may be concerned that the PSI will negatively affect its legitimate commercial shipping and trade.

Some cynical observers suggest that China is trying to protect its strategic interests in a nuclear Pakistan that can hold India in check. They further suggest that it may also be trying to protect its trade in WMD-related materials.[61] But China has questioned the efficiency and legality of the PSI as it involves interdictions, and argued that 'the best way to prevent proliferation of WMD is through dialogue, not force'.[62] Indeed, China's senior expert on arms control Zhang Yan, director-general of the Department of Arms Control and Disarmament in China's Ministry of Foreign Affairs, was quoted as saying 'The PSI has so far failed to completely exclude the possibility of interdiction operations beyond the framework of current international law; that is where China and other countries concerned lies [sic], as well as the major reason why those countries have not joined the PSI.'[63]

China may also be concerned that 'working with PSI countries to halt any North Korean nuclear shipments could negatively affect its role in and effectively scuttle the Six-Party Talks that Beijing is hosting in an attempt to defuse the Korean crisis'.[64] Indeed the PSI has become conflated with the North Korea issue. According to one analyst, 'North Korea insists on an explicit renunciation by the Bush administration of any intent to confront North Korea economically or militarily. But the Bush administration worries that such wording would mean the end of the PSI, at least *vis à vis* North Korea'.[65]

The PSI is of direct relevance to India. Indeed the *Ku Wol San* incident of 30 June 1999 in Kandla was one of those that stimulated the PSI.[66] India's strong naval presence in three high seas areas used for in WMD transportation – the Bay of Bengal, the Indian Ocean and the Arabian Sea – makes it a critical PSI partner, and the United States has pressed India to join the coalition. But this is a difficult decision for India:[67] the PSI is meant in part to enforce the NPT, and India is not a party to the NPT, although it has said it will abide by international non-proliferation norms and India is not at present a country of proliferation concern to the United States. Moreover, if the PSI were to curb proliferation transactions among Pakistan, China and North Korea, it might be in India's interest to join.[68] It could share its intelligence on Pakistani proliferation and gain access to Western intelligence on such transactions.

But these advantages may be outweighed by the disadvantages. Transport of WMD between China and Pakistan could occur across their common land and air border, and shipments between North Korea and Pakistan could move across China's land or air space. Maritime PSI and intelligence sharing would not stop movements along these routes. Furthermore, some Indian analysts think it is unlikely that Indian-supplied intelligence would cause the United States to act against Pakistan's proliferation activities.[69] In India's view the US de-emphasis of Pakistan's involvement in WMD trade undermines the credibility of PSI.[70] Also, it is highly unlikely the coalition would interdict Chinese vessels carrying North Korean shipments to Pakistan, if these were to occur.

More importantly, equipment and materials supporting India's own nuclear programme or its attempts to procure more advanced delivery systems may eventually become the focus of PSI scrutiny and action. It was recently revealed that possible WMD-related electronic components were sent to India through a web of companies in the United States, Israel and South Africa.[71] Further, several Indian companies have allegedly exported sensitive dual-use technology and equipment to 'states of proliferation concern' such as Iraq, making Indian vessels and aircraft potential PSI targets.[72] India also has a strategic cooperation agreement with Iran, which has been named by the US as a 'state of proliferation concern', and is on the verge of finalising contracts for a $4.5 billion natural gas pipeline that will deliver Iranian gas to India.[73] Official PSI participation could also put India at odds with its land a martime neighbours – China, Indonesia and Malaysia – which oppose PSI. Additionally, India would be participating in an activity which, it can be argued, is undermining the UN system, just when it aspires to be part of the leadership of that system. Finally, deployment of naval and air assets for PSI operations may degrade India's warfighting capability vis à vis Pakistan and thus undermine its national security.[74] Thus, it was not surprising that India's Defence Minister Pranab Mukherjee told a January 2005 Asian security conference in New Delhi that although there is a real risk of WMD proliferation through sea-lanes, the PSI proposal needed to be 'examined in greater detail' before India would join.

However, India's parliament did pass a Bill on Weapons for Mass Destruction and their Delivery Systems on 13 May 2005.[75] The legislation, which is now awaiting presidential assent, fulfilled the requirement of UNSCR 1540 by codifying and widening policies and regulations to ensure safety and security of materials and technologies related to WMD and their delivery systems, and it prohibits Indian citizens from manufacturing, transporting, possessing, exporting and brokering WMD. When introducing the bill in Parliament, Foreign Minister K. Natwar Singh reaffirmed that India would remain a nuclear-weapons state.

Although for India the disadvantages of joining the PSI are many and great, some commentators believe it has tacitly joined through the 'back door' by signing a ten-year 'Framework for the US–India Defence Relationship'. The agreement was struck on 28 June 2005 just prior to Prime Minister Manmohan Singh's late July 2005 visit to the United States. The agreement obligates the signatories to 'preventing the spread of WMD' and to enhancing collaboratively their capability to do so.[76] This is only a minor part of the 'Framework', which calls for joint military operations to defeat terrorism, prevent the spread of WMD and protect shipping lanes. In apparent exchange for this agreement, the Bush administration will support the lifting of sanctions imposed on India because of its 1998 nuclear weapons tests, as well as the provision of assistance in expanding its civilian nuclear energy capacity, including dual-use technology.[77] In August 2005, the Bush administration responded to India's concerns regarding discrimination between core PSI participants and others by dismantling the core group. This may make it easier for India to join the PSI publicly.[78] And now that India is contemplating official participation, Pakistan has begun to show interest.[79] Perhaps not coincidentally, the United States has donated to Pakistan 8 P-3c Orion maritime surveillance aircraft, which will be fitted with modern avionics and mission systems by Lockheed Martin Corporation.[80]

On a more practical level, there are questions regarding the PSI's ultimate effectiveness. Despite the growth in participants and supposed successes, the PSI effort is proving complicated in terms of resolving issues of international law, intelligence sharing and operational compatibility. It can be criticised for being disorganised and ineffective, and it has become subject to both domestic politics and the idiosyncrasies of international relations. For example, Spain is not keen on applying the PSI to Iran.[81] A further concern is that there is a lack of appreciation of the threat in both the United States Congress and Europe.[82] And some commentators argue that developments in biotechnology are threatening to render at least current biological and chemical weapons treaties unenforceable. Specifically, the proliferation of new, small, mobile chemical and germ production facilities and new rapid production techniques that replace the need for stockpiling mean that prevention of proliferation may not be possible.[83] Further, the US plan to develop small, low-yield nuclear weapons may prompt others to do the same,[84] and such weapons may be easier to distribute. And the indigenous capability to produce WMD components is spreading rapidly.[85] After all, Iraq's nuclear programme in the 1980s was built with 'dual-use' technology, i.e., technology that also had civilian applications. According to William Perry, former US Secretary of Defense, it is a 'hopeless task' to try and control such technology.[86]

Although the threat of interdiction might deter shipments of the large equipment used to manufacture WMD, it would probably not deter or prevent shipment of small amounts of plutonium.[87] Combinations of planes, trains, or ships carrying WMD material from or to North Korea could link North Korea to other cooperative states by passing through China's territories, or airspace, to and from, e.g., Pakistan. Moreover, the PSI is not concerned only with WMD *per se*, but also with limiting foreign exchange to North Korea, which is allegedly derived primarily from missiles and drug sales.[88] On 29 May 2004, one year after the PSI's initiation, additional shipments of uranium enrichment equipment reached Libya.[89] Obviously the PSI still has serious gaps.

Another problem is that if the PSI begins to be effective, the proliferators are likely to adjust the methods and means of trade in WMD materials.[90] If certain routes are targeted, new routes may be opened. If sea shipments become vulnerable, proliferators may shift to airfreight. Or they may focus more on obtaining WMD design and production knowledge and build them themselves.

PSI effectiveness, particularly vis à vis North Korea, will continue to be limited if key countries like China and South Korea do not participate and if Japan's participation does not expand. The cooperation of India is key but uncertain. For each country, there are certain disadvantages to joining, at least publicly. For the Northeast Asian countries, there is a common desire not to unnecessarily provoke North Korea. Moreover, there is a host practical problems to be overcome. However, if fundamental issues were resolved, key countries might be inclined towards more robust participation.

Fundamental problems

Besides the political and practical problems, there are deeper-seated concerns among developing countries. For example, some feel that the PSI, if carried to its extreme, could further undermine the concept of the sovereignty of nations. The sovereignty of a ship, particularly a government ship, is conceptually akin to that of an embassy in a foreign land. In July 2003, Australian Foreign Minister Alexander Downer said that 'Australia no longer considered the sovereignty of other nations as absolute in international law as it was more important to end humanitarian suffering or security crises'.[91] The United States has already demonstrated this in Kosovo. Indeed, the PSI may become part of the new 'Bush Doctrine' of pre-emptive war, meaning the right to strike anywhere, anytime to protect US security. This may include the prevention of the spread of WMD to countries or groups of concern. The problem of course is that other countries such as North Korea, Australia, India, Russia (vis à vis the Chechens) or even Japan (vis à vis North Korea) may also embrace this doctrine for their own purposes.[92] Indeed, Japan has claimed a right of regional pre-emptive attack.[93] But such action may not be commensurate with Article 2(4) of the UN Charter, which 'prohibits the threat or use of force against the territorial integrity or political independence of any state'.[94]

Other possible repercussions of the PSI include the risk that some states will seek to acquire WMD sooner, before PSI takes full effect; that North Korea will rely more heavily on drug trafficking and counterfeiting for its foreign exchange; that allies will become alienated because of disagreements regarding validity of intelligence, unilateralism and violations of international law; and that international arms control agencies and agreements will be weakened because of diversion of resources and efforts to PSI. There is also concern that if the United Nations is bypassed by PSI interdictions, it also will be further weakened.[95]

The PSI raises a series of fundamental questions, each with considerable significance for international law and global politics. Does the UN Security Council Presidential Statement of January 1992 authorise the use of force to interdict ships on the high seas carrying WMD? If so, should not the UN Security Council make that decision? If not, will the PSI members bring the issue formally before the Security Council? How is a state determined to be 'of concern' and thus have its ships and aircraft subject to interdiction? Who must be concerned and does this 'concern' include commercial trade between states, and commercial vessels sailing under the flag of such states? What is the legal nature of the term 'of concern'? Can any state say that another state is 'of concern' and interdict its ships and planes? Is it legal to interdict on or over the high seas shipments from states not party to the Biological and Toxic Weapons Convention or the Chemical Weapons Convention, or shipments of dual-use chemicals or pathogens? For example, can a country interdict ships or planes of countries such as Israel, India or Pakistan and search their cargo even if, or perhaps because they are not members of the NPT? [96]

America's non-proliferation policy is fraught with apparent contradictions. It seems to say that the United States can develop nuclear weapons for use against small and medium-size states but they cannot in turn develop nuclear weapons of their own.[97] The PSI itself, by seemingly exempting Israel, India and Pakistan, seems to indicate that the United States initiative cares more about who has the weapons than the weapons themselves.[98] As Humayun Khan (a reputed principal in clandestine purchases of high technology components for use in Pakistan's nuclear weapons programme) reportedly said, 'It's all about politics' ... If they don't want us to develop these things, they would do everything they can to stop it ... You [the American government] close one eye and open the other at particular times to these things that have been going on'.[99] Indeed, the United States seems to be suggesting that there is a new class of nations that cannot be trusted with the technology to produce nuclear material, even though the NPT itself makes no such distinction.[100] Having one set of standards for US-friendly nations and another for arbitrarily declared 'rogue' states contradicts the concept of sovereign equality – the principle that all states are entitled to the same rights and protections under international law.

The latest example of these nuclear double-standards is Washington's agreement to allow India to escape the NPT's basic bargain, which allows for provision of technology for civilian nuclear power plants in exchange for renunciation of nuclear weapons.[101] Such nuclear-export restrictions had been imposed on India since it refused to sign the NPT and tested a nuclear weapon using materials and technology from its civilian nuclear power programme. As the *New York Times* said in July 2005, 'A non-proliferation policy that is selective and unilateral is no policy at all'.[102]

There is also concern that 'routine use of preventive war without a demonstrable immediate threat is a corruption of the concept and right of self-defence'.[103] More fundamentally, global acceptance of this unilaterally driven process would indicate a significant change in the framing and implementing of international regulations, constituting 'a major shift from the negotiated multilateralism of the post-war system to cooperative unilateralism under post-Cold War American hegemony'.[104] Indeed John Bolton, appointed US ambassador to the United Nations in August 2005, is now insisting on the right to take unilateral action to prevent the proliferation of WMD.[105]

The PSI relies primarily on force to prevent WMD proliferation.[106] This approach may have some success in the short term but it does not address the root causes of proliferation. The existing international non-proliferation regimes, including the PSI, need to be more balanced and their application more equitable. Their participation should be universal and they should be implemented and enforced through the United Nations.

And there is a fundamental legal dilemma. Without a clear UN resolution or convincing evidence that a shipment is bound for terrorists who intend to use them against the United States, the legality of interdiction of ships on the high seas or even in territorial waters is dubious. To put it bluntly, allowing legitimate commercial transport of WMD components would undermine the objective of the policy. But unilaterally interdicting legal shipments – especially on the high seas, as some analysts believe the United States would like to do[107] – would undermine international law, particularly freedom of navigation, as well as weaken the United Nations. There is an important difference between changing international law and breaking it, although this difference will be perceived variously by different actors. This is the dilemma facing proponents of the PSI. As an indication that the PSI could yet founder on this issue, the Netherlands, one of the original core participants of the so-called 'coalition of the willing', has threatened to withdraw from the PSI if the United States does not ratify the UNCLOS, which guarantees freedom of navigation.[108] Both Norway and Russia have stated that they will not undertake activities that violate international law or their domestic law.[109] Even Australia, a staunch member of the PSI, is undertaking a strategic review of its policies in Asia and the South Pacific that will include an examination of the legality and effectiveness of Australia's involvement in the PSI.[110] Moreover, since China and Russia sit on the UN Security Council, they could block any attempt to change international law to allow such interdictions on the high seas. Thus the PSI and resistance to it may well stimulate a sorely needed rethink and frank discussion of US intentions and their implications for freedom of navigation, the concept of sovereignty, and world order in the twenty-first century. Addressing these fundamental concerns is key to expanding PSI support and participation and thus enhancing its effectiveness.

Conclusions

Although the PSI has made considerable progress through formulating principles of operation, expanding participation and supposedly carrying out successful interdictions, its aggressive promotion and implementation, primarily by the US, has created considerable controversy. It has been criticised for lacking sufficient public accountability, stretching if not breaking the fundamentals and limits of existing international law, undermining the UN system, being limited in its effectiveness and being politically divisive. Moreover, countries that are key to a successful PSI – like China, India, Indonesia and South Korea – have not publicly joined the activity by declaring adherence to its principles, despite US pressure, and Japan and Russia are reluctant participants. For these states, there would be significant disadvantages as well as advantages to public participation, as opposed to covert participation.

The PSI has been cast upon already troubled political seas. In both Northeast and Southeast Asia, Cold War relationships and alliances are being placed under stress as the region's countries re-adjust to each other, the United States, and the new security environment. China's rise, Japan's drive to become a 'normal' country, and big power competition for influence in Southeast Asia provide the political context. Within this context, maritime security issues are rising to the forefront of national concerns. Jurisdiction is creeping seaward and perceptions of threat and concepts of sovereignty are diverging, greatly elevating maritime sensitivities.

Various concerns have limited both PSI participation and its effectiveness. These include a lack of clarity and double standards in PSI definitions, the obligations linked to these vague and subjective definitions, and international legal issues. The latter include possible violation of the regimes of innocent passage and freedom of the high seas, a negative impact on legal trade, and the undermining of both the Law of the Sea and the UN system.

Options for increasing PSI participation and enhancing its effectiveness include changing existing international law; expanding existing conventions or developing a new one; obtaining an unambiguous empowering UN Security Council Resolution; obtaining NATO endorsement; expanding the concept of pre-emptive self-defence; and building a coalition of countries willing to perform such interdictions on each other's ships and aircraft in or over their territorial seas. However each of these options has obstacles and limitations that must be overcome. The PSI has some ways to go before it becomes the widely supported and effective tool its founders envisioned. It requires a sounder rationale and a longer term vision.

Although the PSI was launched with great fanfare and expectations, its progress has been uneven. In reality it is a US-initiated and *ad-hoc* driven activity designed primarily to deter trade in WMD components and 'related materials' to and from North Korea. It suffers from many shortcomings and has limited effectiveness. The secretiveness surrounding PSI interdictions and the methods employed make it difficult to evaluate its success and its legitimacy, and to garner support from countries suspicious of US-driven endeavours. The United States would like to change existing international law to allow PSI interdictions on or over the high seas, either through amendments to the SUA convention or a UNSC resolution, or both, but reaching either objective will be an uphill struggle to gain sufficient support.

Moreover, many countries, including some allies, do not agree with the US argument that such interdictions are warranted by the pre-emptive or preventive war rationale, and do not want the PSI to lead to a diminution of the international prohibition against the use of force.

Further, as often stated by its principal proponents in the United States, the PSI is not an organisation – only an activity – and as such lacks an independent budget or co-ordinating mechanism.[111] Although these features may enhance its flexibility, the speed of decision-making and resultant action, they also constrain its legitimacy and expansion. Moreover, placing such emphasis on interdictions may undermine other non-proliferation efforts.

Perhaps the greatest obstacle to PSI success is the fact that '95 percent of the ingredients for WMD are dual-use in nature, having both civilian and WMD application'.[112] Few if any countries export 'turn-key' WMD. President Musharraf of Pakistan has argued that the A.Q. Khan network only supplied North Korea with centrifuges and that if North Korea has acquired nuclear bomb-making capabilities the North Koreans 'must have got it themselves or somewhere else – not from Pakistan'.[113] The reality is that countries and non-state actors can build their own WMD from dual-use components, using dual-use technologies and machines. This means that it is very difficult to make decisions regarding 'good cause' for interdiction and that such decisions will inevitably be politically influenced and based on who is sending or receiving the shipment. Moreover, a proliferation of interdictions of dual-use materials may hamper legitimate commerce and engender opposition, even from allies.

Disagreements are likely to be exacerbated by the apparent double standards of the current counter-proliferation effort. The United States exempts from the PSI shipments to and from India, Israel and Pakistan for political reasons. And the United States seems to be saying that it can develop nuclear weapons for use against small and mid-size non-nuclear states but they cannot develop such weapons to defend themselves. This makes it more difficult to gather support for the PSI. And state and non-state actors that want to avoid PSI interdictions may move WMD components through non-participating states.

For the PSI to be fully successful will require near-universal support. And even if global support is forthcoming, inadequate resources, intelligence and capacity may ensure that a significant portion of WMD components shipments still avoid detection and air or sea interdiction. Given the PSI's philosophical, legal, political, technical and organisational shortcomings, how can participation and its effectiveness be enhanced?

Enhancing PSI effectiveness
If participation and effectiveness are greatly enhanced, the PSI could become a tremendous addition to the arsenal of anti-proliferation and disarmament regimes. But if its implementation is perceived to be overly zealous, discriminatory, ineffective or illegal, it could be counterproductive. To enhance PSI participation and effectiveness, double standards must be eliminated, transparency increased and a neutral body established to authorise and manage interdictions.

Eliminate double standards. Treatment as sovereign equals is a crucially important principle for smaller nations. To enhance and expand support for the PSI, it is imperative that this principle is applied uniformly and equally to all. To exempt US 'friends' of the moment while targeting unilaterally declared 'rogue states' makes the task of persuading would-be participants that much harder. If the US administration can apply human-rights standards to friends and foe alike, then it ought to be able to apply non-proliferation standards equally as well.

Moreover, the United States should reconsider its own pursuit of tactical nuclear weapons and its failure to ratify the Comprehensive Test Ban Treaty. If the United States truly wants to limit proliferation of WMD, then it needs to lead by example as well as by force. Finally, it should be remembered that, historically, it is companies in the developed world that have knowingly or unknowingly been the principal sources of WMD components, and thus investigations, interdictions and if necessary, sanctions should be applied there equally.

Increase transparency. Presumably, increased transparency would alleviate the growing concern among some key countries and allies regarding the legitimacy of PSI interdictions and the intent of the United States as well, and thus enhance support.

Establish a neutral organisation under UN auspice. Perhaps an 'interdiction committee'[114] is needed to assess intelligence, coordinate and fund activities, including with other non-proliferation instruments and efforts, and to make decisions regarding specific or generic interdictions. Such an organisation, if seen to be neutral, transparent, fair and objective, could answer key questions such as what combinations of actors and materials represent threats and what is 'good cause'? It would also help avoid erroneous judgements and disagreements that might prevent legitimate commerce or delay action. The organisation might have an independent intelligence capability.[115] It would also give the PSI a concrete structure with a consistent strategy and modus operandi, as well as a budget to fill gaps in interdiction and intelligence collection efforts. Moreover it would not supplant or undermine other non-proliferation efforts but instead cooperate with and complement them.

If PSI effectiveness is not dramatically improved, WMD and related materials will continue to fall into the 'wrong' hands. And it may take only one coincidence of will, means and opportunity to create a catastrophe. It is time to move beyond the 'loose arrangement' dominated by the United States. Gains must be consolidated and legitimacy enhanced, thus attracting broader and more robust PSI participation. This could be achieved most effectively by eliminating double standards, increasing transparency and most importantly, providing the PSI with a concrete structure under UN auspices.

NOTES

Introduction

1   'Experts Predict 70pc Likelihood of WMD Attack in Decade', *The New Zealand Herald*, 23 June 2005.

2   'Nonproliferation Initiative Talks Being Held in Paris', http://vilnius.usembassy. gov/pas/hyperFile/evr316.htm

3   Glenn Kessler, 'North Korea May Have Sent Libya Nuclear Material, U.S. Tells Allies', *Washington Post*, 2 February 2005. This allegation may have been false or important information purposefully omitted angering North Korea as well as US allies and casting further doubt on the credibility of US intelligence. Dafna Linzer, 'U.S. Report Blamed for North Korea Impasse', *Washington Post*, 20 March 2005; Jon Wolfsthal, 'Not So Fast', *Nautilus Institute* 10 February 2005.

4   'Five Nations Mulling Pressure on North Korea: NYT'.english.chosun.com, 11 April 2005, http://English.chosun.com/w21data/ html/news/200504/200504100010.html. During an apparent stalemate in the talks, US Secretary of State Condoleezza Rice said that the United States was 'not wholly dependent on negotiation to get this done' and pointedly referred to the PSI. Although the Six-Party Talks appear, as this paper goes to press, to have achieved a breakthrough, the 'devil is in the details'. The chief US negotiator, Assistant Secretary of State Christopher R. Hull, stated at the closing plenary of the fourth round of the talks that 'we should also note on the record that the United States will take concrete actions necessary to protect ourselves and our allies against any illicit and proliferation activities on the part of the DPRK'. This statement raises the interesting question of whether US co-operation or direct involvement in an interdiction of a North Korean vessel under the PSI would constitute an 'attack', an action the United States has affirmed, as part of the six-nation joint statement at the close of the fourth round of talks, it has no intention of taking.

5   Mark T. Esper and Charles A. Allen, 'The PSI: Taking Action Against WMD Proliferation', *The Monitor*, vol. 10, no. 1, spring 2004, p. 4.

6   Timothy Westmyer, 'Congress Seeks Nonproliferation Measures', *Arms Control Today*; 'U.S. Wants Greater Co-operation in WMD Interdiction', *Middle East Newsline*, 9 March 2005; 'U.S. Sets New Defense Strategy,' www.DefenseNews. com, 21 March 2005.

7   John Bolton, Under Secretary for Arms Control and International Security, 'Remarks to the First Anniversary Meeting of the Proliferation Security Initiative', Krakow, Poland, 31 May 2004, http://www. state.gov/t/us/rm/33046.htm

8   *Ibid.*

9   'Proliferation Security Initiative Marks Second Anniversary', www.i-Newswire.

com, 1 June 2005; 'U.S. Intercepts Two Deliveries of Nuclear Material for North Korea', *The Korea Herald*, 2 June 2005.

10 'State's Joseph Urges "Diplomacy of Action" Against WMD Threat', http://usinfo.state.gov/eur/Archive/2005/Aug/17-306543.html

11 'US Promotes Arms Interception Efforts Independent of UN', *New York Times*, 1 June 2005.

12 Barry Schweid, 'Secretary of State Condoleeza Rice Claims Success in Plan to Intercept Weapons Technology', *The Associated Press*, 1 June 2005.

13 Michael Roston, 'Polishing Up the Story on the PSI', *The National Interest*, 9 June 2004.

14 Andrew C. Winner, 'The Proliferation Security Initiative: The New Face of Interdiction', *The Washington Quarterly*, spring 2005, pp. 129–143.

Chapter One

1 Desmond Ball,' A New Era in Confidence Building: The Second-Track Process in the Asia/Pacific Region', *Security Dialogue*, vol. 25, no. 2, 1994, p. 164.

2 The full text of the 1982 UNCLOS can be found here http://www.un.org/Depts/los/convention_agreements/texts/unclos/unclos_e.pdf

3 David I. Hitchcock, Jr., 'East Asia's New Security Agenda', *The Washington Quarterly*, vol. 17, no.1, 1994, pp. 95–96, 103; Paik Jin-Hyun, 'Strengthening Maritime Security in Northeast Asia', paper presented to The 8th Asia-Pacific Roundtable on Confidence Building and Conflict Reduction in the Pacific, ASEAN Institute for Strategic and International Studies, Kuala Lumpur, 5–8 June 1994, pp. 1–17; Stanley B. Weeks, 'Law and Order at Sea: Pacific Co-operation in Dealing with Piracy, Drugs, and Illegal Migration', paper presented to The First Meeting of the CSCAP Working Group on Maritime Co-operation, Kuala Lumpur, June 1995, pp. 1–15; and Charles Meconis and Stanley B. Weeks, 'Co-operative Maritime Security in the Asia-Pacific Region: A Strategic Arms Control Assessment Report', US Department of Defense Report, July 1995, pp. 75–80. For background and specific proposals for cooperation in a variety of maritime sectors, see Joseph P. Morgan and Mark J. Valencia, (eds.), *Atlas for Marine Policy in East Asian Seas*, p. 152; Mark J. Valencia,

(ed.), *International Conference on the Sea of Japan*, Honolulu, East-West Environment and Policy Institute, Occasional Paper no. 3, p. 165; Mark J. Valencia, 'Sea of Japan: Transnational Marine Resource Issues and Possible Cooperative Responses', *Marine Policy*, vol. 14, no. 6, 1990, pp. 507–525; Mark J. Valencia, 'Northeast Asian Perspective on the Security-Enhancing Role of CBMs' in *Confidence and Security-Building Measures in Asia* (New York: Department of Disarmament Affairs, United Nations, 1990), pp. 12–18; and Mark J. Valencia, 'The Yellow Sea: Transnational Marine Resource Management Issues', *Marine Policy*, vol. 12, no. 4, 1988, pp. 382–395.

4 Jack McCafrie and Sam Bateman, 'Maritime Confidence and Security Building Measures in Asia Pacific: Challenges, Prospects and Policy Implications', paper presented to the First Meeting of the CSCAP Working Group on Maritime Co-operation, Kuala Lumpur, June 1995, pp. 1, 11.

5 'Press Briefing by Ari Fleischer, Australia/Terrorism', http://www.whitehouse.gov/news/releases/2002/12/20021202-6.html

6 Achmad Sukarsono, 'Indonesia Being Tested Over Malacca Straits – Report', Reuters, 19 July 2004; '3 Nations Join to Patrol a Vital Oil Lifeline', *International Herald Tribune*, 20 July 2004.

7 Desmond Ball, 'Intelligence Collection Operations and EEZs: The Implications

of New Technology' in Mark J. Valencia and Kazumine Akimoto (eds), *Marine Policy*, Special Issue, Military Intelligence Gathering Activities in Exclusive Economic Zones: Consensus and Disagreement, vol. 28, no. 1, January 2004, pp. 67–82.

8   Mark J. Valencia, 'The Rights of Spy Vessels', *Far Eastern Economic Review*, 11 April 2002.

9   See Appendix I Freedom of Navigation, http://www.fas.org/man/docs/adr_00/apdx_i.htm#top

10 Ser Myo-ja, 'The Alliance: Is It in Trouble', *Joong Ang Daily*, 25 April 2005.

11 It seems that Admiral Fargo was quoted out of context and that there was never any intention of placing US marines in the Malacca Strait, only a desire to assist the Straits countries in technology, equipment, training and intelligence.

12 Sudha Ramachandran, 'Divisions Over Terror Threat in Malacca Straits', *Asia Times Onlilne*, http://www.atimes.com/atimes/Southeast_Asia/FF16Ae01.html

13 Mia Shanley, 'Singapore Allies Stage Security Drill in South China Sea', Reuters, 17 August 2005, http://in.news.yahoo.com/050817/137/5zr7i.html

14 Anthony Tucker-Jones, 'War on Terror Update October 2004', http://www.warshipsiFr.com/pages/terrorism_special12.html

15 Mark J. Valencia, 'Japan in Hot Pursuit of Using Force in Territorial Waters Raises Concerns', *Washington Times*, 25 January 2002, p. A-19.

16 International Tribunal for the Law of the Sea, Judgement of 4 December 1997, http://itlos.org/start2_en.html, paras 155 and 156

17 For an analysis of this incident and the boundary dispute see Jon Van Dyke, Mark J. Valencia and Jerry Miller Garmendia, 'The North/South Korea Boundary Dispute in the Yellow (West) Sea', *Marine Policy*, vol. 27, no. 2, 2003, pp. 143–158.

18 Paul Shin, 'North and South Korea Clash at Sea, Four South Koreans Reported Killed', *Jakarta Post*, Jakarta, Indonesia, 30 June 2002, p. 1.

19 'North Korea Says South Orchestrated Clash in Bid to 'Chill' Reconciliation', *BBC Monitoring Newsfile*, London, 30 June 2002.

20 Seo Hyun-jin, 'Designation of Joint Fishing Area Suggested to Prevent Military Clashes in West Sea', *The Korea Herald*, Seoul, 2 July 2002.

21 Hwang Jang-jin, 'Military Refutes Allegation of Cover-up of June 13 Conflict', *The Korea Herald*, Seoul, 10 July 2002.

22 Don Kirk, 'Sea Clash Leads to Shake Up in Seoul', *International Herald Tribune*, Paris, 12 July 2002.

23 Doug Struck, 'Attack on Boat Premeditated, S. Korea Says, N. Korean Sea Encounters', *The Washington Post*, July 2002.

24 Ministry of Defense, Japan, *Security Outlook 2000*, Tokyo; Ministry of Defense, Japan, *Security Outlook 2001*, Tokyo.

25 Mike Mochizuki and Michael O'Hanlon, 'Put a Lid on Rising Sino-Japanese Tension', *The Japan Times*, 20 April 2005.

26 Reinhard Drifte, '*Japanese-Chinese Security Relations Since 1989*', unpublished manuscript, 2000.

27 'Foreign Minister Kono Questioned by Takemi Keizo at the Foreign Relations and Defense Committee of the Upper House', May 18, 2000.

28 'China Said Conducting Drills in Japan's EEZ', *The Daily Yomiuri*, Tokyo, 26 July 2001.

29 *East Asian Strategic Review 2000*, Tokyo, The National Institute for Defense Studies (NIDS).

30 *East Asian Strategic Review 2002*, Tokyo, The National Institute for Defense Studies (NIDS).

31 *Ibid.*

32 'Chinese Research Ship Spotted in Japanese Waters', *Kyodo News Service*, Tokyo, 1 May 2000; 'Japan Watching Mainland Ship Near Summit Island', *South China Morning Post*, Hong Kong, 23 July 2000.

33 'Japan, China Agreement on Maritime Notice System Detailed', *BBC Monitoring Asia Pacific-Political*, London, 13 February 2001.

Chapter Two

1   The White House, 'National Strategy to Combat Weapons of Mass Destruction', December 2002, http://www.whitehouse.gov/news/releases/2002/12/WMDStrategy.pdf

2   'The Proliferation Security Initiative', http://USinfo.state.gov/is/Archive/2005/May/27-62150.html.

3   Dan Smith, 'The Proliferation Security Initiative: A Challenge Too Narrow', *Foreign Policy In Focus Policy Report*, October 2003, http://www.fpif.org/papers/prolif2003.html

4   Wade Boese, 'The New Proliferation Security Initiative: An Interview with John Bolton', Arms Control Association, 4 November 2003, http://www.armscontrol.org/act/2003_12/PSI.asp; 'Chairman's Statement: Proliferation Security Initiative', PSI Brisbane Meeting, 9–10 July 2003, at: http://www.acronym.org.uk/docs/0307/doc04.htm#01; 'Proliferation Security Initiative: Statement of Interdiction Principles', Paris, 4 September 2003, http://www.proliferationsecurity.info/principles.php

5   Michael Evans and Richard Beeston, 'US Extends Axis of Evil to Syria, Libya, and Cuba', *The Times*, 10 October 2003.

6   Maura Reynolds, 'Libya Decides to Give Up its Banned Arsenal', *Honolulu Advertiser*, 20 December 2003, p 1.

7   Shane Green, 'Pyongyang to Face New Restrictions on Trade', *The Age*, Melbourne, 28 October 2003.

8   Wade Boese, 'The Proliferation Security Initiative: An Interview with John Bolton'. Some analysts claim Robert Joseph, John Bolton's successor at the State Department, was the central figure in creating and building the PSI. Tom Barry, 'Meet John Bolton's Replacement', *CounterPunch*, 15 June 2005.

9   Brisbane Meeting, 9–10 July 2003, 'Chairman's Statement', http://www.dfat.gov.au/globalissues/psi/index.html

10 'U.S. State Department Outlines Proliferation Initiative', 29 December 2004, http://www.allamericanpatriots.com/

11 Chang Z., 'No Legal Grounds for Stopping Ships', *The Korea Herald*, 14 July 2003.

12 John R. Bolton, 'Legitimacy in International Affairs: the American Perspective in Theory and Operation', Remarks to the Federalist Society, Washington DC, 13 November 2003, http://www.state.gov/t/us/rm/26143.htm

13 'Countries Reach Agreement on Interdicting Suspect Cargo', http://www.unwire.org/, 5 September 2003.

14 'North Korea Ships Face More Scrutiny', BBC News World Edition (online), 11 June 2003, http://news.bbc.co.uk/2/hi/asia-pacific/2980418.stm.

15 Indeed it is unclear what precisely is and is not permitted under existing international law. Wade Boese, 'Countries Draft Guidelines for Intercepting Proliferation', *Arms Control Today*, September 2003, http://www.armscontrol.org/act/2003_09/Proliferationinitiative.asp.

16 Remarks by National Security Adviser Dr Condoleezza Rice to the National Legal Center for the Public Interest, The Waldorf Astoria Hotel, New York, 31 October 2003, http://www.whitehouse.gov/news/releases/2003/10/20031031-5.html.

17 Condoleezza Rice, 'PSI: Countering Dangerous Proliferation Worldwide', *The Sunday Times*, 12 June 2005.

18 'US Interdiction Poses Legal Problems', *Oxford Analytica*, 30 June 2003.

19 Virginia Marsh, 'US-led Group Takes to High Seas in First Drill Against WMD Trade', *Financial Times*, 13–14 September 2003, p. 5.

20 David Ensor, 'U.S. to Seize WMD on High Seas', CNN, 2 December 2003, http://www.cnn.com/2003/WORLD/meast/12/02/irankorea.us/

21 'Chairman's Conclusions', Proliferation Security Initiative: London, 9–10 October, *M2 Presswire*, 13 October 2003.

22 David Anthony Denny, 'PSI Seeks to Reduce WMD, Increase Costs of Traffick-

ing', *The Washington File*, 19 December 2003, http://usembassy-australia.state.gov/hyper/2003/1219/epf502.htm.

23 Doug Sample, 'DOD to Use 'Forward-Deployed Active-Layered Defense' to Protect Country', *Air Force Link*, December 2004, http://www.af.mil/.

24 Mark J. Valencia, 'Australia Makes Waves with New Course', *The Straits Times*, 4 March 2005; Michael Wood, 'Australian Maritime Identification System', *The Straits Times*, 16 March 2005; Mark J. Valencia, 'Thrust of Article Valid', *The Straits Times*, 22 March 2005.

25 'U.S. Reveals New Enforcement Capability for Proliferation Security Initiative', *JINSA Online*, 10 February 2005; Michael Wood, 'Australian Maritime Identification System'; Mark J. Valencia, 'Thrust of Article Valid'.

26 Michelle Wiese Bockmann, 'Maritime Zone Plans Scrapped', *The Australian*, 11 July 2005, http://www.theaustralian.news.com.au/common/story_page/0,5744,15887094%255E2702,00.html

27 'Japan Moves Forward to Hinder WMD Smuggling', *The Asahi Shimbun*, 18 July, 2003; 'Korea, Trade Top PM's Agenda', *The Sunday Mail*, 16 July 2003.

28 Robin Wright and Henry Chu, 'Bush Defends Israeli Strike', *Los Angeles Times*, 7 October 2003.

29 'The Proliferation Security Initiative: Statement of Interdiction Principles (adopted in Paris, September 4, 2003)', http://www.state.gov/t/np/rls/other/34726.htm#statement

30 The White House, Office of the Press Secreatary, Proliferation Security Initiative: Statement of Interdiction Principles, 4 September 2003, http://www.state.gov/t/np/rls/fs/23764.htm

31 Specifically, ' the Principles call on all states concerned with this threat to international peace and security to:

1. Undertake effective measures, either alone or in concert with other states, for interdicting the transfer or transport of WMD, their delivery systems, and related materials to and from states and non-state actors of proliferation concern. 'States or non-state actors of proliferation concern' generally refers to those countries or entities that the PSI participants involved establish should be subject to interdiction activities because they are engaged in proliferation through: (1) efforts to develop or acquire chemical, biological, or nuclear weapons and associated delivery systems; or (2) transfers (either selling, receiving, or facilitating) of WMD, their delivery systems, or related materials.

2. Adopt streamlined procedures for rapid exchange of relevant information concerning suspected proliferation activity, protecting the confidential character of classified information provided by other states as part of this initiative, dedicate appropriate resources and efforts to interdiction operations and capabilities, and maximize coordination among participants in interdiction efforts.

3. Review and work to strengthen their relevant national legal authorities where necessary to accomplish these objectives and work to strengthen when necessary relevant international law and frameworks in appropriate ways to support these commitments.

4. Take specific actions in support of interdiction efforts regarding cargoes of WMD, their delivery systems, or related materials, to the extent their national legal authorities permit and consistent with their obligations under international law and frameworks, to include: (a) not to transport or assist in the transport of any such cargoes to or from state or non-state actors of proliferation concern, and not to allow any persons subject to their jurisdiction to do so; (b) at their own initiative, or at the request and good cause shown by another state, to take action to board and search any vessel flying their flag in their internal waters or territorial seas, or areas beyond the territorial seas of any other state, that is reasonably suspected of transporting such cargoes to or from states or

non-state actors of proliferation concern, and to seize such cargoes that are identified; (c) to seriously consider providing consent under the appropriate circumstances to the boarding and searching of its own flag vessels by other states, and to the seizure of such WMD-related cargoes in such vessels that may be identified by such states; (d) to take appropriate actions to (1) stop and/or search in their internal waters, territorial seas, or contiguous zones (when declared) vessels that are reasonably suspected of carrying such cargoes to or from states or non-state actors of proliferation concern and to seize such cargoes that are identified; and (2) to enforce conditions on vessels entering or leaving their ports, internal waters or territorial seas that are reasonably suspected of carrying such cargoes, such as requiring that such vessels be subject to boarding, search, and seizure of such cargoes prior to entry; (e) at their own initiative or upon the request and good cause shown by another state, to (a) require aircraft that are reasonably suspected of carrying such cargoes to or from states or non-state actors of proliferation concern and that are transiting their airspace to land for inspection and seize any such cargoes that are identified; and/or (b) deny aircraft reasonably suspected of carrying such cargoes transit rights through their airspace in advance of such flights; (f) if their ports, airfields, or other facilities are used as transshipment points for shipment of such cargoes to or from states or non-state actors of proliferation concern, to inspect vessels, aircraft, or other modes of transport reasonably suspected of carrying such cargoes, and to seize such cargoes that are identified.' *Ibid.*

32 C. Raja Mohan, 'Dismantling Core Group, US Eases India's Path to Proliferation Security', *The Indian Express*, 18 August 2005, http://www.indianexpress.com/full_story.php?content_id=76505

33 Proliferation Security Initiative Frequently Asked Questions (FAQ), Fact Sheet, Bureau of Nonproliferation, US Department of State, 26 May 2005, http://www.state.gov/t/np/rls/fs/46839.htm

34 Ye Ru'an and Zhao Qinghai, 'The PSI: Chinese Thinking and Concern', *The Monitor*, vol. 10, no. 1, spring 2004, p. 23.

35 Stephen G. Rademaker., Assistant US Secretary of State for Arms Control, 'Testimony before the House Internal Relations Committee', Subcommittee on International Terrorism and Nonproliferation', Washington DC, 9 June 2005, http://www.state.gov/t/ac/rls/rm/47715.htm

36 *Ibid.*

37 *Ibid.*

38 Edward Harris, 'Liberia OKs U.S. Ship Searches', *Associated Press*, 14 February 2004.

39 Wade Boese; 'Countries Draft Guidelines for Intercepting Proliferation'; Wade Boese, 'Key US Interdiction Initiative Claim Misrepresented', *Arms Control Today*, July/August 2005, http://www.armscontrol.org/act/2005_07-08/Interdiction_Misrepresented.asp.

40 Caitlin Harrington, 'Pentagon Reveals Navy Will Board Suspected Terror Ships', *CQ Homeland Security-Border Security*, 26 May 2004, www.cq.com.

41 Jacquelyn S. Porth, 'Experts Meet in Omaha to Consider Ways to Disrupt WMD Transfer', *Washington File*, 21 March 2005.

42 Ralph A. Cossa, 'Proliferation Security Initiative', *Korea Times*, 23 October 2003.

43 'Multilateral Maritime Interdiction Exercise Begins', http://www.news.navy.mil/index.asp, 16 October 2003.

44 'Japan to Send Observers to International Maritime Inspection Drill', *Financial Times*, 21 November 2003.

45 John R. Bolton, 'Remarks at Proliferation Security Initiative Meeting', Paris, http://www.state.gov/t/us/rm/23801pF.htm, 4 September 2003 http://www.state.gov/t/us/rm/23801.htm

46 There are three types of PSI meetings: 1. Plenary meetings of all PSI core participants (Bolton maintains there is no

'membership' as such because there is no organisation to belong to);

2. Exercises attended by only some of the core participants and sometimes by non-declared participants; and

3. Meetings of Operational Group of Experts (OEG).

47 'London Talks Study Beefing Up Fight Against Traffic in WMD', *Agence France Presse*, 10 October 2003.

48 Greece, New Zealand and Thailand joined the PSI in 2005. Jacquelyn S. Porth, 'Experts Meet in Omaha to Consider Ways to Disrupt WMD Transfer'. In April 2004, the Czech Republic formally joined the PSI. Yann-hui Song, 'An Overview of Regional Responses in the Asia-Pacific to the PSI in Countering the Spread of Weapons of Mass Destruction: The Role of the Proliferation Security Initiative', *Issues and Insights*, vol. 4, no. 5, Pacific Forum CSIS, July 2004, pp. 7–31. In a 16 September 2005 speech to a UNSC summit, Philippine President Gloria Macapagal declared Philippine support for the PSI. Michaela P. del Callar, 'Gloria, with Big Mike Around, Courts US Support in UN Meet', *The Daily Tribune On the Web!* (Manila), http://www.tribune. net.ph/headlines/20050916.head04.html

49 'Four New Nations to Join US-led Non-proliferation Scheme', 2 December 2003, Agence Presse-France, cited on http://www.spacewar.com/2003/ 031202225431.7m405hmo.html.

50 'Gaining Momentum: Plan to Seize Weapons in Transit', *Straits Times Interactive*, 19 December 2003; Barry Schweid, 'Officials Work to Block Weapons Transfers', *The Associated Press*, 17 December 2003.

51 'U.S. to Practice Weapons Interdiction Near North Korea Missile Seizure Site', *Associated Press*, 19 December 2003.

52 'Anti-WMD Interdictions Reach Three', http://www.news.com.au/, 16 January 2004.

53 Office of the Press Secretary, The White House, 'Proliferation Security Initiative:

Statement of Interdiction Principles, Fact Sheet'.

54 'US to Host International WMD Drill', http://www.abc.net.au/news/, 11 July 2004.

55 *Ibid.*

56 'Proliferation Security Initiative Marks Second Anniversary', http://i-newswire. com/, 1 June 2005; 'U.S. Intercepts Two Deliveries of Nuclear Material for North Korea', *The Korea Herald*, 2 June 2005.

57 Assistant Secretary of State Stephen Rademaker, 'Testimony Before the House International Relations Subcommittee on International, Terrorism and Nonproliferation, 9 June 2005.

58 'Bulgaria Joins Proliferation Security Initiative', *Sofia News Agency*, 2 June 2005.

59 Eric Watkins, 'Japan Urges Malacca Straits Shipping Safety,' *Oil and Gas Journal*, 21 January 2005.

60 Jacquelyn S. Porth, 'Experts Meet in Omaha to consider ways to Disrupt WMD Transfer'.

61 '19 Navies Test Command System in Singapore', The Malaysian National News Agency, http://bernama.com/, 18 May 2005.

62 Dominique Loh, 'Proliferation Security Exercise Ends with Inspection of Suspected Vessel', Channel News Asia, 18 August 2005, http://www.channelnewsasia. com/stories/singaporelocalnews/ view/163885/1/.html; Mia Shanley, 'Singapore, Allies Stage Security Drill in South China Sea', 17 August 2005, http:// in.news.yahoo.com/050817/137/5zr7i.html

63 Melinda Larson and Kathryn Whittenberger, 'U.S., Southeast Asia Navies Work Toward Common Goal During SEACAT', www.news.navy.mil, 1 June 2005.

64 Juliana Gittler, 'U.S. Begins High-Seas Anti-Terrorism Games', *Stars and Stripes*, 6 June 2005.

65 Alexander Pojedinec, 'Proliferation Security Initiative: Two Years and Counting', Center for Defense Information Report, 1 August 2005, http://www.poni-csis.org/ file.asp?F=PSIReport%2Epdf&N=PSIRepo

rt%2Epdf&C=articles. The estimate of 64.5 incidents a year includes only materials related to nuclear weapons programmes and not chemical or biological weapons and only known incidents. Thus, the average may be much higher, making the eleven successful interdictions minuscule by comparison.

66 Toby Warrick, 'On North Korean Freighter, a Hidden Missile Factory', *Washington Post*, 14 August 2003, p A1.

67 'US Interdiction Poses Legal Problems', *Oxford Analytica*.

68 Jason Chudy, 'NATO Group Exercise Included USS Taylor', *Stars and Stripes*, 29 May 2005.

69 Martin Bright *et al.*, 'Hunt for 20 Terror Ships', *Observer* (London), 23 December 2001. p 1.

70 'U.S. Warning: Navy Will Attack Any 'Hostile Ship' ', *Lloyd's List*, 21 March 2003.

71 'Indian-US Joint Naval Exercises Begin', *BBC Monitoring International Reports*, 6 October 2003.

72 Brian Reyes, 'Show of Force: NATO Troops Monitor Maritime Traffic in the Mediterranean to Prevent Terrorists Using Ships', *Lloyd's List*, 3 June, 2003; Brian Reyes, 'Security – NATO Forces Board Two Ships in Mediterranean', *Lloyd's List*, 7 May 2003.

73 'Canadian Ship to Join Campaign Against Terrorism in Arabian Gulf', *Canada News Wire Group*, 9 March 2005.

74 White House Press Office, 'Text of Letter from President Bush to the Speaker of the House of Representatives and the President Pro Tempore of the Senate', Press Release, 20 May 2005. http://www.whitehouse.gov/news/releases/2005/05/20050520-8.html

75 'Al Qaeda's "Navy" – How Much of a Threat', Center for Defense Information, 20 August 2003, http://www.cdi.org/friendlyversion/printversion.cfm?documentID=1644

76 David Sanger and Thom Shanker, 'Reluctant U.S. Gives Assent for Missiles to Go to Yemen', *New York Times*, 12 December 2002, pp. A1 and A20; William McMichael, 'Coalition Crews Intercept Ship with Hidden Warheads', *Navy Times*, 23 December 2002, pp 24–25.

77 Press Briefing by Ari Fleisher, 11 December 2002, http://www.whitehouse.gov/news/releases/2002/12/20021211-5.html.

78 J. Ashley Roach, 'Initiatives to Enhance Maritime Security at Sea' in Mark J. Valencia and Kazumine Akimoto (eds), 'Military and Intelligence Activities in Exclusive Economic Zones: Consensus and Disagreement', *Marine Policy*, Special Issue, vol. 28, no. 1, January 2004, pp. 41–66; Ruth Wedgewood, 'A Pirate is a Pirate', *Wall Street Journal*, 16 December 2002, p A12; also see Frederic L. Kirgis, 'Boarding of North Korean Vessel on the High Seas', *ASIL Insights*, 12 December 2002, http://www.asil.org/insights/insigh94.htm.

79 Safa Haeri, 'WMD Transport Targeted on High Seas', *Asia Times*, 12 September 2003.

80 CNNcom./WORLD,24 June 2003, http://edition.cnn.com/2003/WORLD/europe/06/23/greece.ship/

81 Helena Smith,' Nato "Terror" Tip Off on ExplosivesShipSailingtoSudan',*Guardian*, 24 June 2003, http://www.guardian.co.uk/alqaida/story/0,12469,983876,00.html

82 Yoo Yong-won, 'Spain Seized Arms Shipment Called Legal', *Digital Chosen*, 2 July 2003; Yoo Yong-won, 'Spain Suspects Gun Find Destined for Ivory Coast', *Reuters*, 2 July 2003.

83 'S. Seeks Further Taiwan's Cooperation for Regional Security', *Kyodo News Service*, 26 August 2003.

84 Barry Schwied, 'U.S. Blocked Centrifuge Parts for Libya', *Associated Press*, 31 December 2003; Robin Wright, 'U.S. Details Seizure of Libya-bound Cargo', *The Washington Post*, 1 January 2004; David E. Sanger, 'Month of Talks Fails to Bolster Nuclear Treaty', *The New York Times*, 28 May 2005; Michael Roston, 'Polishing Up the Story on the PSI', *In The National Interest*, 9 June 2004.

Chapter Three

1   These terms have been defined in the Draft Resolution introduced to the UN Security Council as follows:
    'Definitions *for the purpose of this resolution only:*
    Means of delivery: missiles, rockets and other unmanned systems capable of delivering nuclear, chemical, or biological weapons, that are specially designed for such use.
    Non state actor: individual or entity, not acting under the lawful authority of any State in conducting activities which come within the scope of this resolution.
    Related materials: materials, equipment and technology covered by relevant multilateral treaties and arrangements, or included on national control lists, which could be used for the design, development, production or use of nuclear, chemical and biological weapons and their means of delivery.'
    'Draft Resolution on Non-Proliferation', introduced to the UN Security Council by the United States of America and the United Kingdom of Great Britain and Northern Ireland, 24 March 2004. However it is not clear that the PSI uses the same definitions.

2   Michael E. Beck, 'The Promise and Limits of the PSI', *The Monitor,* vol.10, no. 1, spring 2004, pp. 16–17.

3   Ye Ru'an and Zhao Qinghai, 'The PSI: Chinese Thinking and Concern', *The Monitor,* vol. 10, no. 1, spring 2004, p. 23.

4   'U.S. State Department Outlines Proliferation Security', 29 December 2004, http://www.allamericanpatriots.com/.

5   Proliferation Security Initiative Frequently Asked Questions (FAQ), Fact Sheet, Bureau of Nonproliferation, US Department of State, 26 May 2005.

6   Barbara Demick, 'CIA Lists North Korea as a Nuclear Country', *Honolulu Advertiser,* 9 November 2003, p A8.

7   Dafna Linzer and Anthony Faiola, 'U.S. Won't Confront Seoul on Nuclear Tests', *Washington Post,* 25 November, 2004.

8   Wayde Boese, 'The Proliferation Security Initiative: an Interview with John Bolton', *Arms Control Today,* 3 December 2003.

9   Andrew C. Winner, 'The Proliferation Security Initiative: The New Face of Interdiction', *The Washington Quarterly,* vol. 28, no. 2, spring 2005, pp. 129–43.

10 Based on UNCLOS, Article 106, 'Liability for seizure without adequate grounds'.

11 *Ibid.*

12 *Ibid.*

13 John R. Bolton, 'Legitimacy in International Affairs: the American Perspective in Theory and Operation', Remarks to the Federalist Society, Washington DC, 13 November 2003.

14 United Nations, Official Text of the United Nations Convention on the Law of the Sea, United Nations, New York, 1983, Article 19, http://www.un.org/Depts/los/convention_agreements/texts/unclos/closindx.htm.

15 Natalino Ronzitti, 'The Law of the Sea and the Use of Force Against Terrorist Activities', *in* Natalino Ronzitti (ed.), *Maritime Terrorism and International Law,* (New York: Kluwer Law International, 1990), pp 1–15; Benjamin Friedman, 'The Proliferation Security Initiative: The Legal Challenge', *The Bipartisan Security Group,* 4 September 2003, http:gsinstitute.org/gsi/pubs/09_03_psi_brief.pdf

16 'Treaty on Non-proliferation of Nuclear Weapons', Article I, http://www.fas.org/nuke/control/npt/text/npt2.htm

17 Jofi Joseph, 'The Proliferation Security Initiative: Can Interdiction Stop Proliferation', *Arms Control Today,* June 2004.

18 Thom Shanker, 'U.S. Remains Leader in Global Arms Sales, Report Says', *New York Times,* 25 September 2003, Section A, p 12.

19 David Krieger and Devon Chaffee, 'Facing the Failures of the Nuclear Non-Proliferation Treaty Regime', *Institute for Energy and Environmental Research* website, April 2003.

20   Ron Hutcheson, 'Libya Thaw May Yield Intelligence Booty', *Honolulu Advertiser*, 21 December 2003.

21   Zahid Hussain, 'Pakistan Opens Weapons Probe Nuclear-program Architect is Targeted and Evidence of Links to Iran and Libya', *Asian Wall Street Journal*, 24 December 2003.

22   Douglas Frantz, 'Israel Subs Can Launch Nuclear Missiles', *Los Angeles Times*, 12 October 2003.

23   'Japan Plans to Develop Missile Components with US', *Daily Times*, 18 October 2004; 'Japan Could Sell New Missiles: Ono', *The Japan Times*, 15 July 2005.

24   Mark Trevilyan, 'Ship En Route to Iran Tests WMD Proliferation Deal', *Reuters*, 26 April 2005.

25   United Nations, UNCLOS, Article 108; Testimony by Rear Admiral John E. Crowley, Chief Counsel and Judge Advocate General, United States Coast Guard, Committee on Foreign Relations, 21 October 2003, Federal Document Clearing House Congressional Testimony.

26   Natalino Ronzitti, 'The Law of the Sea and the Use of Force Against Terrorist Activities', p. 5.

27   The Bush administration supports accession of the United States to the Convention. 'Statement by Admiral James D. Watkins, Chairman, US Commissioner Ocean Policy, before the Committee on Senate Foreign Relations', 14 October 2003, Washington DC, Federal Document Clearing House, Congressional Testimony.

28   Devon Chafee, 'Freedom or Force on the High Seas: Arms Interdiction and International Law', 15 August 2003, Institute for Energy Environment Research, http://www.ieer.org/.

29   Doug Wrenn, 'L.O.S.T. Treaty Appropriately Named', *Magic City Morning Star* (Millinocket, Maine) 27 January 2005; Frank Gaffney, 'Freedom at Sea Too', *The Washington Times*, 25 January 2005; Paul M. Weyrich, 'Sovereignty Under Siege by International Sea Treaty', 12 January 2005, http://www.gopusa.com/; Oliver North, 'The Trojan Horse on America's Shores', GOPUSA, 1 April 2005.

30   Statement by the President, 10 March 1983, http://www.un.org/Depts/los/LEGISLATIONANDTREATIES/PDFFILES/USA_1983_Statement.pdf

31   Daniel H. Joyner, 'The PSI and International Law', *The Monitor*, vol. 10, no. 1, spring 2004, pp. 7–9.

32   Takao Hishinuma, 'U.S. May Down Aircraft Thought to Carry WMD', *Daily Yomiuri*, 19 December 2003.

33   Natalino Ronzitti, 'The Law of the Sea and the Use of Force Against Terrorist Activities', p 12.

34   *Ibid.*

35   Raghu, 'Where Have All the WMDs Gone?', *People's Democracy* [weekly newspaper], vol. 28, no. 8, 22 February 2004; Stuart McMillan, 'US Tackles 'Rogue States' Nuclear Weapons', *New Zealand National Business Review*, 20 February 2004.

36   'Remarks by US Secretary of Defense Donald Rumsfeld at the International Institute for Strategic Studies Shangri-La Dialogue' (Singapore), *DOD News*, 9 June 2004.

37   Michael Byers, 'Policing the High Sea; the Proliferation Security Initiative', *The American Journal of International Law*, vol. 98, no. 526, July 2004, pp. 1–19.

38   Andreas Persbo and Ian Davis, 'Sailing into Uncharted Waters? The Proliferation Security Initiative and the Law of the Sea', British American Security Information Council Research Report 2004.2, May 2004, http://www.basicint.org/pubs/research/04PSI.htm

39   Michael Roston, 'Polishing Up the Story on the PSI', *In the National Interest*, 9 June 2004, http://www.inthenationalinterest.com/Articles/Vol3Issue23/Vol3Issue23Roston.html; Alexander Pojedinec, 'Proliferation Security Initiative: Two Years and Counting', 28 July 2005, http://www.cdi.org/pdfs/psi-2yrs.pdf

40   Kari Huus, 'Plan to Cut Off N. Korea Takes Shape', 20 October 2003, http://www.msnbc.com/news/924919.asp?cp1=1.

41 'A Decade of Deception and Defiance', 12 September 2002, http://www.rrojasdatabank.org/pfpc/decade.pdf

42 Security Council Resolutions, http://www.un.org/Docs/scres/2001/sc2001.htm

43 Robert A. Hamilton, 'International Maritime Expert: Law Supports War on Terror – German Law School Vice Dean Speaks to Coast Guard Class', *The Day*, 9 November 2003, http://theday.com/eng/web/

44 'US Measures for Combating Terror', *East African Standard* (Nairobi), 14 July 2003.

45 The Uniting for Peace Resolution is a method adopted by the UN Security Council in 1950 to ensure that stalemates between members of the Security Council would not prevent the UN from maintaining international peace and security. It provides that if, due to lack of unanimity on the Security Council, the UN cannot maintain peace because of a threat to the peace, breach of peace, or act of aggression, the UN General Assembly will consider the matter immediately. It has been used ten times including in 1956 against France and Britain's occupation of the Suez Canal and to pressure the Soviet Union to leave Hungary. Michael Ratner and Jules Lobel, 'A UN Alternative to War': "Uniting for Peace"', http://www.casi.org.uk/discuss/2003/msg01158.html

46 *Ibid.*

47 Beth Jinks, 'US Worked with IMO on Maritime Security Measures', *The Business Times* (Singapore), 11 February 2003.

48 Mark Turner, 'US Drafts UN Move to Reduce Flow of Weapons', *Financial Times*, 18 December 2003.

49 Colum Lynch, 'U.S. Urges Curb on Arms Traffic', *Washington Post*, 25 March 2004, p A20.

50 Maggie Farley, 'Resolution Seeks Ban on Spread of Weapons', *Los Angeles Times*, 29 April 2004.

51 Ralph Cossa, 'Introduction' in 'Countering the Spread of Weapons of Mass Destruction: the Role of the Proliferation Security Initiative', *Issues and Insights*, vol. 4, no. 5, Pacific Forum CSIS, July 2004, pp. 1–6, http://www.csis.org/pacfor/.

52 'U.S. State Department Outlines Proliferation Security', http://www.allamericanpatriots.com/, 29 December 2004.

53 UN Security Council Resolution 1540, 28 April 2004, http://www.state.gov/t/np/rls/other/31990.htm; Center for Nonproliferation Studies, Monterey, 'United Nations Security Council Resolution 1540, May 2005, http://www.nti.org/f_wmd411/f2n.html

54 Evelyn Leopold, *Reuters*, 25 March 2004.

55 William Varner, 'Pakistan Leads Opposition at UN to Terrorism Measure', *Bloomberg*, 5 April 2004; *Daily Times* (Lahore), editorial, 1 May 2004.

56 Jofi Joseph, 'The Proliferation Security Initiative: Can Interdiction Stop Proliferation?', *Arms Control Today*, June 2004.

57 US Department of State, Fact Sheet, Bureau of Nonproliferation, Washington DC, 26 May 2005, http://www.state.gov/t/np/rls/fs/46839.htm

58 *Ibid.*

59 Wade Boese, 'US Nonproliferation Resolution Advances at UN', *Arms Control Today*, April 2005.

60 'Security Council, Briefed by Chairman of Anti-Terrorism Committees; Call for Strengthened Cooperation, Enhanced Information Sharing', http://i-newswire.com/, 26 April 2005.

61 'Pakistani Indicted in Nuclear Sales', *Honolulu Advertiser*, 9 April 2005, p. A5; Josh Meyer, 'Illegal Nuclear Deals Alleged', www.latimes.com, 26 March 2005. It has now been revealed that the A.Q. Khan network supplied North Korea with centrifuges for enriching uranium as well as their designs. 'Pakistani Expert Gave N. Korea Nuke Parts', *The Star* (Penang, Malaysia), 26 August 2005, p. 36.

62 Foreign Policy Association, *Proliferation Security Initiative: Principles and Practices*, 7 September 2003, http://www.fpa.org/.

63 'World Leaders Urged to Act Boldly', *Financial Express* (New Delhi), 22 March 2005.

64 'Listen to Annan', *International Herald Tribune*, 26 September 2003, p. 8.

65 John R. Bolton, 'Remarks at Proliferation Security Meeting', Paris, France, http://www.state.gov/t/us/rm/23801.htm

66 Bill Gertz, 'Rumsfeld Pushes "new sense of urgency"', *Washington Times*, 24 October 2003.

67 John R. Bolton, 'Remarks at Proliferation Security Meeting'.

68 'Rice: U.S. Has Not Lost Patience With Six-Party Talks', http://english.chosun.com/, 27 April 2005.

69 'N Korea May Face Nuclear Dragnet', *The Australian*, 13 May 2005; David Sanger, 'White House May Go to U.N. Over North Korean Shipments', *New York Times*, 25 April 2005.

70 'US Mulls New Strategies Against North Korea', http://channelnewsasia.com/, 23 March 2005.

71 Benjamin Friedman, 'The Proliferation Security Initiative: The Legal Challenge'.

72 Nunn–Lugar Cooperative Threat Reduction Act of 2005 (Introduced in the Senate), S 313 IS, 109th Congress, 1st Session, 8 February 2005, Library of Congress, http://thomas.loc.gov/

73 Ted L. McDorman, 'From the Desk of the Editor-in-chief', *Ocean Development and International Law*, vol. 35, 2004, pp. 379–384.

74 John Duff, 'A Note on the United States and the Law of the Sea: Looking Back and Moving Forward', *Ocean Development and International Law*, vol. 35, 2004, pp. 195–219.

75 United Nations Convention on the Law of the Sea, signed at Montego Bay, Jamaica, 10 December 1982, Part VII, Article 88, http://www.un.org/Depts/los/convention_agreements/texts/unclos/closindx.htm

76 'Different Perspectives on the Issues', in *The Regime of the Exclusive Economic Zone: Issues and Responses*, A Report of the Shanghai Meeting, Ship and Ocean Foundation, Tokyo 2005, pp. 46–61.

77 Convention for the Suppression of Unlawful Acts Against the Safety of Maritime Navigation, 1988, http://www.imo.org/Conventions/mainframe.asp?topic_id=259&doc_id=686

78 J. Ashley Roach, 'Initiatives to Enhance Maritime Security at Sea', in Mark J. Valencia and Kazumine Akimoto (eds), 'Military and Intelligence Gathering Activities in Exclusive Economic Zones: Consensus and Disagreement', *Marine Policy*, Special Issue, vol. 28, no. 1, January 2004, pp. 41–66.

79 International Chamber of Commerce (ICC), 'Pirate Attacks Against Ships Increase', 24 October 2002, http://www.iccwbo.org/; J. Ashley Roach, 'Initiatives to Enhance Maritime Security at Sea' , p. 3; Jay Batongbacal, 'Trends in Anti-Piracy Cooperation', paper presented to the Okazaki Institute, March 2001, p. 125; 'Nuclear Brinkmanship Tests US Resolve', *Oxford Analytica*, 16 December 2002.

80 Michael Richardson, 'It's Full Steam Ahead in Hunt for Terror Arms Shipments', *Straits Times*, 26 October 2003.

81 'UK Outlines Plans to Counter WMD Trafficking', *Xinhua News Agency*, 25 February 2004.

82 'Japan Eyes Changes to Convention to Allow WMD Searches at Sea', *Asia Pulse*, 27 January 2005.

83 Michael Evans, 'US Plans to Seize Suspects at Will', *The Times*, 11 July 2003; 'SUA Review Continues as Legal Experts Tackle Security', *IMO News*, 2002, no. 4, p. 16.

84 'Report of the Legal Committee on the Work of its Eighty-Seventh Session', International Maritime Organization, Legal Committee, 87th Session, Agenda Item 17, 23 October 2003.

85 'Legal Committee (LEG) 88th Session', http://www.imo.org/index.htm, 19–23 April 2004.

86 Amendments to Suppression of Unlawful Acts (SUA) Treaties Set for Adoption in October 2005, IMO Legal Committee 89th Session, 25–29 October 2004; 'IMO to Review Draft Amendments of SUA Convention and Protocol', *Taiwan News Online*, 27 June 2005, http://www.etaiwannews.com/

87 *Ibid.*

88 Andrew J. Grotto, 'Lack of American Leadership Impeding Nonproliferation Efforts', *Center for American Progress*, 19 August 2004, http://www.americanprogress.org/site/c.biJRJ8OVF/b.8473/.

89 'US Planning to Sign up More Countries to Curtail Weapons Sale', http://www.xinhuanet.com/english/, 11 September 2003.

90 Benjamin Friedman, 'The Proliferation Security Initiative: The Legal Challenge'.

91 'New Command; Continuing Tensions', *Oxford Analytica*, 16 June 2003.

92 Carol Gioacomo, 'U.S. Won't Back off North Korea', *Reuters*, 22 October 2003.

93 'Treaty on the Non-Proliferation of Nuclear Weapons', Article 1, http://www.un.org/Depts/dda/WMD/treaty/.

94 Howard LaFranchi, 'Bush in Asia: All About Security', *The Christian Science Monitor*, 20 October 2003.

95 'US Concerned by Syria's WMD Capabilities', *Scoop*, 17 September 2003; Bob Edwards, 'Training Exercises by 11 Nations to Perform Mock Aerial Interceptions of Weapons of Mass Destruction', *US National Public Radio*, 12 September 2003.

96 Vanessa Gera, 'Iran to let U.N. into Nuclear Facilities', *Honolulu Advertiser*, 19 December 2003, p. A9.

97 George John, 'Iran Reaffirms Nuclear Program Pledges', *Honolulu Advertiser*, 9 November 2003; Ali Akbar Dareini, 'Iran Authorizes Signing of Pact Calling for Nuclear Inspecting', *Honolulu Advertiser*, 11 December 2003, p. A10; Vanessa Gera, 'Iran to Let U.N. into Nuclear Facilities', *Honolulu Advertiser*, 19 December 2003, p A9.

98 Douglas Frantz, 'Israel Subs Can Launch Nuclear Missiles', *Los Angeles Times*, 12 October 2003.

99 'Japan Concerned about US Plan to Make 'Small' Nuclear Arms', *Kyodo News Service*, 25 November 2003.

100 Mohamed ElBaredi, '7 Steps for Preventing Nuclear Proliferation', http://www.asahi.com/english/, 16 February 2005.

101 Dafna Linzer, 'U.S. Reverses Position on Weapons Inspections', *Washington Post*, 1 August 2004.

102 G. Parthasarathy, 'Nukes in the New World Order', *The Pioneer* (New Delhi), 30 June 2005.

103 David E. Sanger, 'Month of Talks Fails to Bolster Nuclear Treaty', *The New York Times*, 28 May 2005.

104 Stephen Zunes, 'Missile Love in Pakistan', http://www.fpif.org/index.htm, June 2005.

105 'A Blow to the NPT', editorial, *The Japan Times*, 1 June 2005.

106 Anticipatory self-defence is an attack upon another state which actively threatens violence and has the capacity to carry out the threat but has not yet done so; preventive self-defence is an attack against another state when a threat is feared or suspected but there is no evidence that the threat is imminent. Daniel H. Joyner, 'The PSI and International Law'.

107 John Kerin, 'Net Tightens on North Korea – Australia Part of 'Fast Track' Coalition to Intercept Suspect WMD Ships', *The Australian*, 11 July 2003.

108 Benjamin Friedman, 'The Proliferation Security Initiative: The Legal Challenge'.

109 'The Dossiers', http://dossiers.genfoods.net/bwarcrimes.html; The White House, 'III. Strengthen Alliances to Defeat Global Terrorism and Work to Prevent Attacks Against Us and Our Friends' ,14 September 2001, http://www.whitehouse.gov/nsc/nss3.html

110 Gerald F. Seib, 'A Bush Doctrine is Put in Jeopardy by Weapons Hunt', *Asian Wall Street Journal*, 9 October 2003.

111 'U.S. May Allow Nuke Strikes Over WMD', *The Japan Times*, 2 May 2005.

112 Dale Eisman, Maritime Leaders Named to Joint Chiefs of Staff', *The Virginia Pilot*, 23 April 2005, http://home.hamptonroads.com/stories/story.cfm?story=85463&ran=57470

113 Gerald F. Seib, 'A Bush Doctrine is Put in Jeopardy by Weapons Hunt'; Robert

A. Hamilton, 'International Maritime Expert: Law Supports War on Terror'.

[114] *Ibid.*

[115] 'Charter of the United Nations', Chapter VII, Breaches of the Peace and Acts of Aggression, Article 51, http://www.un.org/aboutun/charter/.

[116] 'Report of the Secretary General's High-Level Panel on Threats, Challenges and Change', 2 December 2004, http://www.un.org/secureworld/report.pdf

[117] 'Fight on WMDs Boasts Global Backing', *The Washington Times*, 23 December 2005.

[118] 'World Leaders Urged to "Act Boldly"', *Financial Express* (New Delhi), 22 March 2005.

[119] Michael Byers, 'Policing the High Sea; the Proliferation Security Initiative'.

[120] Robert Block, 'U.S. to Require Advance Notice on Cargo Update', *Asian Wall Street Journal*, 24 November 2003.

[121] John Kerin, 'War on Terror's Shipping Focus', *The Honolulu Advertiser*, 17 July 2003.

[122] Michael Richardson, 'It's Full Steam Ahead in Hunt for Terror Arms Shipments'; 'U.S. Eyes Pact to Allow More Vessel Inspections', *The Daily Yomiuri*, 28 October 2003, p. 2.

Chapter Four

[1] 'Terrorism Joins Piracy as Shipping Threat', *Oxford Analytica*, 3 February 2003.

[2] Mark Husband, 'Shipping is "Wide Open" to Terror Threat', *Financial Times*, 10 October 2003.

[3] David Krieger and Devon Chafee, 'Facing the Failures of the Nuclear Non-proliferation Treaty Regime', 23 April 2003, http://www.wagingpeace.org/articles/2003/04/23_krieger_npt-failures.htm.

[4] Bush State of the Union Address, 29 January 2002, http://archives.cnn.com/2002/ALLPOLITICS/01/29/bush.speech.txt/

[5] Jofi Joseph, 'The Proliferation Security Initiative: Can Interdiction Stop Proliferation', *Arms Control Today*, June 2004.

[6] 'U.S. Steps Up Pressure on Pyong Yang', *Chosun Ilbo*, 15 February 2005.

[7] Wade Boese, 'Interdiction Initiative Starts to Take Shape', *Arms Control Today*, http://www.armscontrol.org/act/2003_10/InterdictionInitiative.asp, 2 October 2003; Barbara Slavin, 'Exercise Aims to Inhibit North Korean Arms Trade', *USA Today*, 9 September 2003; 'Bye-bye Bolton', www.WorldNetDaily.com, 8 January 2005; 'Preventing Nuclear Terrorism

is a Responsibility of Each Nation', *Washington File*, 18 March 2005.

[8] Ralph Cossa, 'Proliferation Security Initiative' *The Korea Times*, 23 October 2003.

[9] Carla Anne Robbins, 'Why U.S. Sidestepped U.N. in Its Plan to Halt Shipment of Weapons', *Asian Wall Street Journal*, 23 October 2003, p. A6.

[10] David Hughes, 'Flag States Need to Fulfill Duties in Era of Global Terrorism', *The Business Times (Singapore)*, 25 February 2004; 'Board and Search WMD Initiative Strengthened by Deal with Liberia', www.Townhall.com, 13 February 2004.

[11] Michael Richardson, 'To Disrupt and Deter', *Defense Technology Asia*, 30 April 2004.

[12] Carol J. Williams, 'Panama to Sign Shipping Accord', *The Los Angeles Times*, 12 May 2004;

[13] *Ibid.*

[14] 'Cyprus US Reach Agreement on PSI', *China View*, 11 April 2005; 'The United States and the Republic of Cyprus Proliferation Security Initiative Ship Boarding Agreement', http://i-newswire.com/pr38245.html

[15] 'The United States and the Republic of Croatia Proliferation Security Initiative Shipboarding Agreement', http://i-news-

wire.com/pr23367.html, 3 June 2005; 'The United States and Belize Proliferation Security Initiative Ship Boarding Agreement', http://i-newswire.com/goprint40572.html.

16 'Terrorism and Weapons Proliferation on the High Seas', *STRATFOR*, 16 February 2004; 'UK Outlines Plans to Counter SMC Trafficking', *Xinhua News Agency*, 25 February 2004.

17 'US Wants Nations to Deny Overflight Rights to Suspected WMD Traffickers', *Agence France Presse*, 5 March 2004.

18 Anonymous, 'NORAD May Turn Its Eyes', http://www.gazette.com/, (Colorado Springs), 15 January 2005.

19 Chief of Naval Operations Public Affairs, 'CNO 2005 Guidance Plots Navy's Course', press release, 7 January 2005.

20 Bill Gertz, 'New US Center to Check Spread of WMD', *Washington Times*, 29 June 2005.

21 'Beginning to Transform the State Department to Meet the Challenges of the 21st', http://I-newswire.com/goprint39118.html

22 Dafna Linzer, 'U.S. Plans New Tool to Halt Spread of Weapons', *Washington Post*, 27 June 2005, http://www.washingtonpost. com/wp-dyn/content/article/2005/06/26/ AR2005062601336.html; Gordon Prather, 'Freezing Assets on a Whim', http://www. worldnetdaily.com/, 2 July 2005.

23 Wade Boese, 'United States Eyes Proliferations' Assets', *Arms Control Today*, 8 September 2005.

24 Lewis Dunn, 'Proliferation Security Initiative (PSI) – What, What Not, Why, What Next *in* Countering the Spread of Weapons of Mass Destruction: The Role of the Proliferation Security Initiative', *Issues and Insights*, vol. 4, no. 5, Pacific Forum CSIS, July 2004, pp. 36–39.

25 John Kerin, 'Allies Want Russia and China in WMD Hunt', *The Australian*, 16 September 2003; Guy Dinsmore and Andrew Ward, 'US Lobbies Russia and China on Curbing WMD', *Financial Times*, 10 September 2003, p.13.

26 Brendan Pearson, 'Tokyo Treads Warily on Use of Interdiction Force', *Australian*

Financial Review, 12 July 2003; Takashi Ono and Yoshiro Mino, 'Japan Nervous as Star of WMD Exercise', *Asahi Shimbun*, 15 September 2003.

27 Patrick Goodenough, 'China Opposes Pressure on North Korea: Wants Resumption of Talks', http://www. cnsnews.com/, 16 July 2003; Samantha Maiden, 'War Possible to Halt Nuclear Threat', *Honolulu Advertiser*, 14 July 2003.

28 Paul Kern, 'North Korea Nuclear Talks: If at First You Don't Succeed, Meet Again', *Arms Control Today*, 20 June 2004.

29 Hidemichi Katsumata, 'MSDF Fuels Sea War on Terrorism', *Daily Yomiuri*, 30 April 2004.

30 Speech by Minister of State for Defense Shigeru Ishiba at the IISS Asia Security Conference Singapore, 5 June 2005, Shangri-la Dialogue, International Institute for Strategic Studies.

31 Daisuke Kajimoto, 'Proliferation Security Initiative – A Case Study of US–Japan Alliance Cooperation within the Coalition of the Willing', unpublished manuscript, The Henry L. Stimson Center, 19 October 2004.

32 'Outlines of Additional War Contingency Bills Decided', *Kyodo News Service*, 23 February 2004; Nao Shimoyachi, 'Final Bills on Attack Response Await OK', *The Japan Times*, 25 February 2004; 'Bill Eyed for Ship Checks at Sea', *Yomiuri Shimbun*, 30 January 2004; 'Anticipation of an armed attack' means a country is indicating its intention to attack Japan by force, and is massing its vessels or aircraft for this purpose, or fuelling a rocket for launching a missile; a certain country is calling up its reservists and is banning outside activities of important military personnel in order to attack Japan, and is building new military facilities for attacking Japan', 'Xinhua Analyzes Japan's Motives in Enacting "Emergency Legislation"', Xinhua, 6 June 2003.

33 This was part of a package of War Contingency Bills. Maeda Hisao, 'The 2002 Defence Ministry White Paper. Full

Speed Ahead to the National Warfare State', *Japan Focus,* http://japanfocus.org/article.asp?id=018

34 'Lead Cabinet Member Endorses Additional War Contingency Bills', *Xinhua,* 9 March 2004; 'Japan Boosts Powers for Military Emergencies', *New York Times,* 7 June 2004.

35 Tai Hwan Lee, 'China and Japan: a Korean Perspective' paper presented to the Sejong-SAIS Workshop on 'Korea, the United States and Northeast Asia', 11–12 November 2004, Seoul, Korea..

36 'Spy Catches: On Guard: Two Special Patrol Forces Comb the Seas for Intruders', *The Asahi Shimbun,* 23 February 2004.

37 'Japan to Hold Sea Drill to Stop WMD Smuggling', *Asahi Shimbun,* 27 July 2004.

38 Daisuke Kajimoto, 'Proliferation Security Initiative – A Case Study'.

39 *Ibid.*

40 Takehiko Yamamoto, 'Japanese Engagement in the PSI', *The Monitor,* vol. 10, no. 1, spring 2004, pp. 20–22.

41 The exercise scenario: Japan receives intelligence of a suspected chemical weapons-related shipment on a Japanese-flagged ship (*Yokohama Autumn*) scheduled to come to port in Japan and the shipment is subsequently transferred to an American-flagged ship (*American Summer*) sailing towards Japan. Both ships are on the high seas. The Japan Self Defense Forces and coast guard maritime patrol aircraft track the ships. The Japanese coast guard boards the Japanese flagged vessel, finds the illicit cargo, and directs the Japanese ship to port. Japanese authorities direct Australian, US and French vessels to the US flagged ship, which is subsequently boarded. Japanese authorities assist in identifying the transferred shipment, which is subsequently identified as illicit cargo and seized. Fact Sheet, Bureau of Nonproliferation, US Department of State, 22 October 2004.

42 Jong-Heon Lee, 'Analysis: North Korea Raises the Stakes', *United Press International,* 6 May 2005.

43 'Full Text of Joint U.S. – Japan Security Committee Statement', *CNA News,* 21 February 2005, http://www.channelnewsasia.com/

44 'New Japan, U.S. Roles Eyed', *Yomiuri Shimbun,* 18 May 2005.

45 Eric Watkins, 'Japan Urges Malacca Strait Shipping Safety', *Oil and Gas Journal,* 21 January 2005; 'SDF Sending Armed Unit to Terror Drill', *Asahi Shimbun,* 16 August 2005, p. 22; Speech by MR Teo Chee Hean, Minister for Defence, at the Opening Ceremony of Exercise Deep Saber, 15 August 2005.

46 'Ono: SDF Plans to Join WMD Drill', *Asahi Shimbun,* 6 May 2005.

47 Carol Giacomo, 'U.S. Presses Russia to Join Arms Body', *The Moscow Times,* 29 January 2004, p 3.

48 'Russian Diplomat Says Interception Training May Prolong Nuclear Crisis', ABC News Radio online (Australia), 11 September 2003.

49 *Ibid.*

50 Sergie Blagot, 'Russia Hesitant to Endorse US' "Greater Middle East Initiative"', *The Daily Star* (Beirut), 7 June 2004.

51 Young-Sik Kim, 'Russia Attempted to Stop North Korea's Missile Export', http://www.donga.com/, 28 January 2005.

52 Joe Fiorill, 'IAEA Questions Iranian Centrifuge Program, Uranium Traces, More', *Global Security Newswire,* 2 June 2004, http://globalsecuritynewswire.org

53 James Cotton, 'The Proliferation Security Initiative and North Korea: Legality and Limitations of a Coalition Strategy', *Security Dialogue,* vol. 36, no. 2, June 2005, pp. 193–211.

54 Kim Ki-tae, 'Jeong on US to Soften on NK', *Korea Times,* 2 October 2003; 'Next Round of Korean Talks to Start as Early as June 23', *Reuters,* 10 June 2004.

55 Ryu Jin, 'S. Korea Reluctant to Join US-Led Security Initiative', *Korea Times,* 2 May 2005.

56 James Cotton, 'The Proliferation Security Initiative and North Korea'.

57 Safa Haeri, 'WMD Transport Targeted on High Seas', *Asia Times,* 12 September 2003.

58 'Rumsfeld to Visit China, Eyes Hot Line for Defense', *Washington Times*, 9 February 2005.

59 Michael Richardson, 'Between a Rogue and a Hyperpower', *South China Morning Post*, 12 December 2003, p. 17.

60 'Uranium Elemental to China Trade Leap', *Sydney Morning Herald*, 17 March 2005.

61 Mohan Malik, 'Nuclear Proliferation and A.Q. Khan's China Connection', *Association for Asia Research*, 26 May 2004, http://asianresearch.org/articles/2066. html.

62 'Countries Reach Agreement on Interdicting Suspect Cargo', http://www. unwire.org/, 5 September 2003; 'China Voices Concern Over WMD Non-proliferation Plan's Legality', 9 December 2003, as quoted in Andreas Persbo and Ian Davis, 'Sailing into Uncharted Waters? The Proliferation Security Initiative and the Law of the Sea', BASIC Research Report 2004, 2 June 2004, http://www. basicint.org/pubs/Research/04PSI.htm

63 Edward Lanfranco, 'China Won't Sign On To PSI', Asia -Pacific News, Monsters and Critics.com, 2 September 2005, http://news.monstersandcritics.com/ asiapacific/printer=104550.php

64 Michael Richardson, 'It's Full Steam Ahead in Hunt for Terror Arms Shipments', *Straits Times*, 26 October 2003, http://straitstimes.asia1.com.sg/

65 David E. Sanger, 'US and Two Allies Agree Plan for North Korea', *New York Times*, 8 December 2003.

66 Toby Warrick, 'On North Korean Freighter a Hidden Missile Factory', *Washington Post*, 14 August 2003, p. A1.

67 'US Security Initiative: An Invitation to India Cannot be Turned Down', *The Times of India,* 14 October 2003; G. Balachandran, 'The new US Non-proliferation Initiative and India', *The Financial Express* (New Delhi), 27 October 2003; 'The New U.S. Non-proliferation Initiative and India', *The Financial Express* (New Delhi), 26 October 2003.

68 *Ibid.*

69 G. Balachandran, 'The New US Non-Proliferation Initiative and India'.

70 Subhash Kapila, 'India Should Not Join Proliferation Security Initiative (PSI)', South Asia Analysis Group, 4 January 2004, http://www.saag.org/papers10/paper969.html

71 'Pakistani Indicted in Nuclear Sales', *Honolulu Advertiser*, 9 April 2005. p. A5.

72 Jofi Joseph, 'The Proliferation Security Initiative'

73 Gordon Prather, 'US Proliferation Rhetoric and Reality', http://www.antiwar.com/ prather/?articleid=6691, 18 July 2005.

74 Seema Mustafa, 'India Surrenders Ocean to US', *The Asian Age*, 4 July 2005.

75 'Russia, India, Algeria, Poland, Turkey Address Disarmament Conference Nuclear, Other Issues', http://www.i-newswire.com/, 6 June 2005.

76 Praful Bidwai, 'Eyes Wide Shut, India Enters Military Alliance with U.S.', Inter Press News Agency, 4 July 2005; Praful Bidwai , 'Charter of Dependence', 19 July 2005, http://in.rediff.com/news/2005/jul/19bidwai.htm.

77 'India-US Agree on Eight Major Initiatives', http://www.newkerala.com/ news.php?action=full, 19 July 2005.

78 C. Raja Mohan, 'Dismantling Core Group, US Eases India's Path to Proliferation Security', *The Indian Express*, 18 August 2005, http://www.indianexpress.com/print. php?content_id=76505. On 25 September 2005, as this paper went to press, India and the United States began their largest-ever joint naval exercise, *Malabar-05*, a ten-day exercise involving almost 10,000 personnel from the two countries. *Malabar-05* will include maritime interdiction and VBSS operations focused on piracy and terrorism. Although such interdictions are the heart of PSI and the Indian Navy is keen to join it, Indian officials deny that the exercise is realted to the PSI. 'Biggest Indo-US Naval Exercise', *The Times of India Online*, 24 September 2005, http://timesofIndia. indiattimes.com/articleshow/msid-1241308,pvtpage-1.cms; 'No PSI Element

in Naval Drills with U.S.', *The Hindu*, 25 September 2005, http://www.thehindu.com/2005/09/25/stories/200592502711000.htm

79 'Pakistan Reviewing Proliferation Initiative', *Daily Times* (Lahore), 19 August 2005, http://www.dailytimes.com.pk/default.asp?page=story_19-8-2005_pg7_40

80 'Pakistan Acquires US P-3C Surveillance Aircraft', *Reuters*, 31 August 2005, http://www.khaleejtimes.com/displayArticle.asp?col=&section=subcontinent&xfile=data/subcontinent/2005/August/subcontinent_August1130.xml

81 Carla Anne Robbins, 'Why U.S. Sidestepped U.N. in Its Plan to Halt Shipment of Weapons'.

82 Office of the Press Secretary, the White House, 'Proliferation Security Initiative: Statement of Interdiction Principles, Fact Sheet, 4 September 2003', http://www.state.gov/t/np/rls/fs/23764.htm

83 Judith Miller, 'Arms Control Racing Time and Technology', *New York Times*, 6 December 2003.

84 'Japan Concerned about US Plan to Make 'Small' Nuclear Arms', *Kyodo News Service*, 25 November 2003.

85 Jofi Joseph, 'The Proliferation Security Initiative'.

86 Stephen Zunes, 'Missile Love in Pakistan', *Foreign Policy In Focus Project*, June 2005.

87 Anonymous, 'North Korea's Proliferation Activities Said to Have Limits', http://www.PolitInfo.com/, 28 December, 2004. Since 1981, Israel has been in violation of UNSCR 487, which calls on Israel to place its nuclear facilities under the trusteeship of the IAEA. Since 1998, Pakistan and India have been in violation of UNSCR 1172 calling on these nations to end their nuclear weapons programs and eliminate their long-range missiles. Yet only Iraq was targeted for strict sanctions and military action for its violation of UNSC resolutions. Stephen Zunes, 'Missile Love in Pakistan'.

88 Mark Husband, 'Shipping is 'Wide Open' to Terror Threat', *Financial Times*, 10 October 2003.

89 Michael Roston, 'Polishing Up the Story on the PSI', *In The National Interest*, 9 June 2004.

90 Andrew C. Winner, 'The Proliferation Security Initiative: The New Fact of Interdiction', *The Washington Quarterly*, vol. 28, no. 2, spring 2005, pp. 129–143.

91 Malcolm Cole, 'Think-tank Shapes World View', *Courier Mail* (Brisbane), 10 July 2003.

92 Yong Tiam Kui, 'Australia, North Korea, Join Pre-emptive Bandwagon', *New Straits Times*, 26 October 2003, p. 4.

93 Richard Tanter, 'Japanese Militarization and the Bush Doctrine', *Japan Focus*, 15 February 2005, http://www.japanfocus.org/article.asp?id=221

94 Charter of the United Nations, http://un.org/aboutun/charter/

95 Carla Ann Robbins, 'Why U.S. Sidestepped U.N. in Its Plan to Halt Shipment of Weapons'.

96 Thomas Graham and Jonathan Grassoff, Foreward to Ben Friedman, 'The Proliferation Security Initiative: the Legal Challenge', Bipartisan Security Group, Global Security Group, 11 September 2003.

97 'Encouraging Nuclear Proliferation', editorial, *New York Times*, 10 February 2005.

98 'Web Exclusive, John Bolton Would Rather Keep America Free of Commitments than Keep the World Free of Nuclear Weapons', *The American Prospect*, 7 April 2005, http://www.prospect.org.

99 Josh Meyer, 'Illegal Nuclear Deals Alleged', www.latimes.com, 26 March 2005.

100 'Bush Seeks to Alter Global Nuclear Pact', *International Herald Tribune*, editorial, 16 March 2005.

101 'Green Light for Bomb Builder', *New York Times*, editorial, 22 July 2005.

102 *Ibid*.

103 Dan Smith, 'The Proliferation Security Initiative: A Challenge Too Narrow', *Foreign Policy in Focus*, October 2003.

104 David Rosenberg, 'Dire Straits: Competing Security Priorities in the So8uth China Sea; 13 April 2005.

105 Gordan Prather, 'Bolton in a China Shop', *Worldnetdaily*, 3 September 2005, http://worldnetdaily.com/news//article.asp?ARTICLE_ID=46122

106 Ye Ru'an and Zhao Qinghai, 'The PSI: Chinese Thinking and Concern'.

107 'Harsh Words and Rhetoric Aren't Enough', *Oxford Analytica*, 22 March 2005.

108 Joan Lowry, 'Oceans Treaty May Interfere with Weapons Initiative', *Scripps Howard News Service*, 27 May 2004, http://www.shns.com/shns/g_index2.cfm.

109 Andew Prosser, 'The Proliferation Security Initiative in Perspective', www.cdi.org/pdfs/psi.pdf

110 'Australia to Reexamine Regional Security', ABC Online, 13 April 2005, http://www.abc.net.au/

111 Andrew Prosser, 'The Proliferation Security Initiative in Perspective'.

112 Michael E. Beck, 'The Promise and Limits of the PSI', *The Monitor*, vol. 10, no. 1, spring 2004, pp. 16–17.

113 'Pakistan Expert Gave N. Korea Nuke Parts', *The Star* (Panang, Malaysia), 26 August 2005, p. 36.

114 Andreas Persbo and Ian Davis, 'Sailing into Uncharted Waters'.

115 Michael E. Beck, 'The Promise and Limits of the PSI', pp. 16–17.

ADELPHI PAPERS

The Adelphi Papers monograph series is the Institute's flagship contribution to policy-relevant, original academic research.

Eight Adelphi Papers are published each year. They are designed to provide rigorous analysis of strategic and defence topics that will prove useful to politicians and diplomats, as well as academic researchers, foreign-affairs analysts, defence commentators and journalists.

From the very first paper, Alastair Buchan's 'Evolution of NATO' (1961), through Kenneth Waltz's classic 'The Spread of Nuclear Weapons: More May Be Better' (1981), to influential additions to the series such as Mats Berdal's 'Disarmament and Demobilisation after Civil Wars' (1996) and Lawrence Freedman's 'The Revolution in Strategic Affairs' (1998), Adelphi Papers have provided detailed, nuanced analysis of key security issues, serving to inform opinion, stimulate debate and challenge conventional thinking. The series includes both thematic studies and papers on specific national and regional security problems. Since 2003, Adelphi Paper topics have included 'Strategic Implications of HIV/AIDS', 'Protecting Critical Infrastructures Against Cyber-Attack', 'The Future of Africa: A New Order in Sight', 'Human Rights and Counter-terrorism in America's Asia Policy', 'Somalia: State Collapse and the Threat of Terrorism', 'Counter-terrorism: Containment and Beyond', 'Japan's Re-emergence as a "Normal" Military Power', and 'Weapons of Mass Destruction and International Order'.

Longer than journal articles but shorter than books, Adelphi Papers permit the IISS both to remain responsive to emerging strategic issues and to contribute significantly to debate on strategic affairs and the development of policy. While the format of Adelphi Papers has evolved over the years, through their authoritative substance and persuasive arguments recent issues have maintained the tradition of the series.

RECENT **ADELPHI PAPERS** INCLUDE:

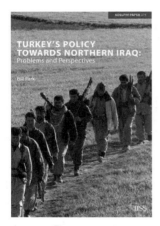

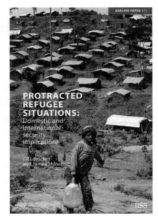

ADELPHI PAPER 374

Turkey's Policy Towards Northern Iraq: Problems and Perspectives

Bill Park

ISBN 0-415-38297-1

ADELPHI PAPER 375

Protracted Refugee Situations: Domestic and international security implications

Gil Loescher and James Milner

ISBN 0-415-38298-x